THE DUTCHMAN BOLD
The Story of
ABEL TASMAN

THE DUTCHMAN BOLD

The Story of
ABEL TASMAN

GEORGE FINKEL

Angus and Robertson

Portrait used in cover design was taken from (NK 3) Cuyp, J. G. Abel Tasman, his wife and daughter. Oil 42" × 52". Rex Nan Kivell Collection in the National Library of Australia.

First published in 1975 by
ANGUS AND ROBERTSON (PUBLISHERS) PTY LTD
102 Glover Street, Cremorne, Sydney
2 Fisher Street, London
159 Boon Keng Road, Singapore
P.O. Box 1072, Makati MCC, Rizal, Philippines
115 Rosslyn Street, West Melbourne
222 East Terrace, Adelaide
1 Little Street, Fortitude Valley, Brisbane

National Library of Australia
card number and ISBN 0 207 13113 9

Printed in Great Britain by
Northumberland Press Ltd
Gateshead

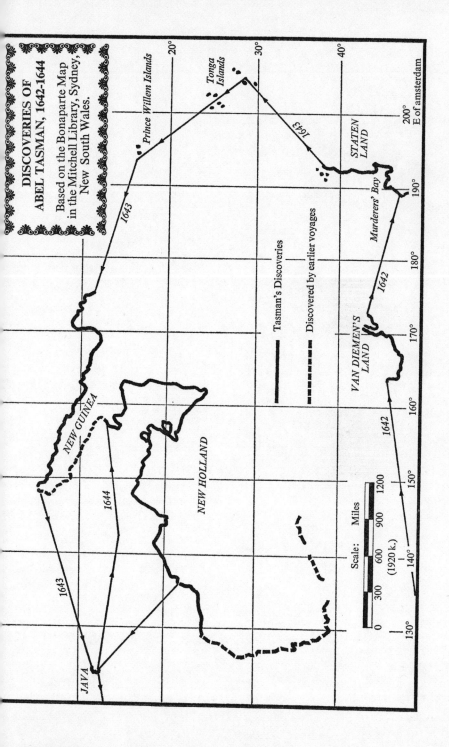

DISCOVERIES OF
ABEL TASMAN, 1642-1644

Based on the Bonaparte Map
in the Mitchell Library, Sydney,
New South Wales.

Tasman's Discoveries
Discovered by earlier voyages

Scale: Miles
0   300   600   900   1200
(1920 k.)

NEW GUINEA

NEW HOLLAND

JAVA

VAN DIEMEN'S
LAND

STATEN
LAND

Murderers' Bay

Tonga
Islands

Prince Willem Islands

1642
1643
1644

20°
30°
40°

130° 140° 150° 160° 170° 180° 190° 200°
E of amsterdam

Contents

Servant of the Company

1

Decision

ABEL JANSZOON TASMAN was ill at ease as he stood by the communion table in Amsterdam Old Kirk waiting for Jannetie. It was cold on that January Sunday in 1632, for all that the tiled stoves at either end of the building shimmered with heat. His starched linen collar was choking him, and the new shoes with their cut steel buckles were cramping his feet. Abel almost wished he were at sea in smock and sea boots, since here he could scarcely swing his arms across his chest to bring some feeling back into his hands.

Jannetie Tjaerss was late. Claesgie, his first wife, had not been early either. It was odd how time dragged or sped according to how it was being spent. He had not been in the church more than ten minutes, but it seemed as long as an uneventful sea watch on a cold night.

Abel looked at Gerrit Demmer, the groomsman, standing beside him. Some time he must remember to ask Gerrit about this time-speed thing, since he had a philosophical turn of mind and always enjoyed a good discussion.

The precentor came from the vestry, looking sourly at Abel as if it were his fault that the bride was late. Abel glared back. The precentor was not the only one wishing the ceremony over.

Abel's thoughts strayed to Claesgie who had died after the birth of their daughter three years ago. At the time he had been on a voyage to Riga for a cargo of naval stores. He remembered how sweetly the ship had smelt of tar and sawn pinewood on the passage back. Sometimes, even now,

3

a whiff of that smell reminded him sharply that he was a widower with a daughter.

It had been hard, at first, to realize that little Claesgen was his own. If he could have seen her in her mother's arms just once, it would have been different. But that was a sailor's life—two years of happiness ashore with Claesgie, then three years of widowhood. And now he was to wed again.

He did not need a wife as much as Claesgen needed a mother. Abel came from Lutjegast, near Groningen, and had no relatives in Amsterdam to look after his daughter. A child needed a settled home, such as he had known when a boy; and this was what Jannetie would help to provide.

He shifted his chilled feet, and sighed inwardly. He would never feel towards Jannetie as he had felt towards Claesgie. But he was very fond of her, and they would get on well enough, for all that his heart did not sing on meeting her as it had done with Claesgie.

There was a stir at the far end of the church, and Abel felt a draught as the leather door-curtain shifted. Half turning to look, he felt Gerrit touch his sleeve to remind him that it was bad luck to look upon the bride until she was beside him. He had turned to smile at Claesgie, he remembered suddenly, and she had motioned for him to look away. Heavens! Could this be the reason she had died?

Who could tell? If he had not signed on for the voyage to Riga, he could have been at home for the birth. But even then he would not have had the money to pay the midwife. Money didn't go far these days, after sixty-odd years of Spanish Wars. Maybe, if he had not been a seaman, Claesgie would have lived. But if he hadn't been a seaman, he would never have met her, for Groningen was a long way from Amsterdam.

The pastors said the pattern of life was spun by the fingers of God. Then it was God who had decided that Claesgie should die, and his marriage to Jannetie was also

4

God's will. Abel suddenly felt very small, as he sometimes did on a summer night watch, with the stars set out overhead like jewels on the inside of a velvet-lined bowl. He saw the pastor approaching with the book in his hand, and felt a small stirring at his side. Jannetie had come at last.

The wedding breakfast was held at the house in Teerketel Lane, and in no time the place was crowded with well-wishers come to drink their health. As was customary, they had walked home from the church, little Claesgen between her father and stepmother. Her face was solemn, and her hands were carefully tucked into an otter-skin muff—a gift brought back by her father from one of his voyages.

It was after midnight when the last guest departed, and next day was rather flat. Jannetie's sister, Giertie, came round to help with the clearing-up, or it would have been flatter still. Abel felt restless, because the *Maria Danz*, on which he was signed, was refitting, and there was little for him to do, apart from the occasional anchor watch. He could sleep at home four nights out of five.

They were sitting by the stove that evening when Jannetie looked up from her knitting. 'You will be sailing away again soon, husband?'

'What would you have me do, since I'm a seaman by trade?'

'I do not complain, Abel. If men like you did not follow the sea, the city and the States-General would be ruined. But there was something Gerrit Demmer said yesterday: that both you and he are qualified to ship as mates. I did not know this.'

'Gerrit's right. And so are another half-dozen of us in the *Maria Danz* qualified. But mates' berths are hard to come by, unless you have a share in a ship. And how would I get the money for that?'

'How much money would you need?'

'About a thousand guilders.'

'More than three years' pay! It would take a deal of saving.'

'Ah, Jannetie, we could never save that much. But there's always a chance—maybe salvage or prize-money.'

'Chance is a broken-winded horse, as my father often says. Still, let's hope it comes your way.'

Abel laughed as he relit his pipe. 'The way things are just now I'm lucky to be in a berth before the mast. There are plenty glad to go as paid hands in the herring fleets— and that's blood for money.'

'Trade is bad because of the wars, they say.'

'That's only part of the truth. The wars are making some people rich. We've had war in the Netherlands for sixty years now, and there are those who will blame them for everything, from a bad harvest to a cold in the head. The simple fact is that there are too many seamen for the amount of trade.'

'Well, I can see no cure for that.'

'A man could go where there was a chance of developing a good trade, and a few ships to carry it.'

Jannetie rummaged in her knitting-bag for more wool. 'Is there such a place?'

'Over in the Americas there's New Amsterdam. There's not much doing there yet, and it would be a harder life than here until a colony was established.'

'Yet it might be worth it. Are there any others?'

'There's the Indies, East and West.'

'But there are pirates in those parts.'

'There are pirates everywhere, even in the North Sea. Gerrit and I once thought of going out to the East Indies.'

'But you've never been there. Why not?'

'Mainly because of Claesgen. As it is, much of the winter I spend at home, and I'm ashore every few weeks during the rest of the year, so she doesn't grow up to forget me.'

'And if you went to the East?'

'Service with the Dutch East India Company means signing a three-year contract, not counting the passage out and home—say four years in all. Claesgen would have quite forgotten me while I was away, and that's too high a price to pay for a mate's berth!'

In mid February the *Maria Danz* sailed across to Leith, but she was embayed in the Forth by a series of spring gales, which meant Abel was away longer than usual. It was early in April before he saw Amsterdam again.

A few days after Abel's return he and Jannetie spent an evening with the Demmers, leaving Claesgen tucked up in bed with a neighbour's children. It was fresh April weather, with a slight chill in the air after a warm day. Birds were mating, and trees were swelling into leaf; it was a day to stir the blood with the promise of summer.

Gerrit Demmer was taller than Abel, dark-haired against the other's thick-set fairness. Gerrit's family were of Huguenot stock and had migrated to the Provinces after the Bartholomew Massacres in 1572. Amsterdam was tolerant of religion, so long as the citizens paid their taxes. Jews and Christian sects lived side by side, agreeing to differ on matters of faith and showing a united front to outside interference.

'A fine evening, Abel,' said Gerrit, when Margrethe, his wife, had taken Jannetie into the bedroom to take off her wraps.

'Indeed, and a world away from the foul weather we had in the North Sea.'

Gerrit poured out schnapps. The friends tossed the spirits down their throats at a swallow, Abel shuddering slightly as the fiery stuff bit into his stomach.

'I've often wondered what makes the sadness I feel on a spring evening,' said Gerrit, putting his glass down on the table.

'You are more of a philosopher than I, Gerrit. Is there an answer to that?'

'I don't know of one, unless it is that spring reminds me of being a year older, and still in the same rut.'

'What rut? We're seamen, not ploughboys! A month ago we were drinking ale in Scotland.'

'What was so different about that? We went back on board to sleep in the same fo'c'sle and eat with the same messmates! The Scots are not so different from us—and their kirk is exactly the same.'

'I heard that, Gerrit,' said Margrethe, coming from the bedroom. 'You are still on the old topic, that everything is always the same.'

'Well, isn't it?'

'I don't see it that way,' said Abel. 'You remember the day we crossed the Forth on the ferry, to Kirkcaldy?'

'I do, and a freezing day it was.'

'I've known it colder, just as I've known better towns than Kirkcaldy. But it was different from any place over here. There are hills in that country, near Kirkcaldy, but they are farther off.'

'There are hills, and some of them are high, but I still say one hill is very like another.' Gerrit's voice was quite firm.

'Maybe, but you cannot be sure of that. We have never reached the higher ones, nor seen the other side. A country on one side of the sea is different from a country on the other; you must admit that. So that what lies on the far side of a hill may be quite unlike what lies on the near side.'

'Heavens, Abel, and you say I am a philosopher!'

'It must be a fine thing to be a man,' Margrethe said to Jannetie. 'Imagine having a day with nothing to do but walk over these hills, wondering whether it was forest or polder on the far side.'

'Margrethe, you don't understand. A man has to do something in a foreign port.'

'Maybe so. But women never get to see more than the view from the kitchen window.'

'Well, we once talked about going to the Indies. That would at least give you a different kitchen, and a different view to look at.'

'And it would be one way of getting a mate's berth,' said Abel. 'Jannetie and I talked about this not long ago.'

'I would go wherever Abel went,' said Jannetie. 'He knows that, and it is for him to make the decision.'

'One would certainly see the far side of a lot of oceans and hills,' said Abel, 'and that's something I've always hankered after.'

'And a mate's berth to go with it,' said Gerrit.

'With a share in the ship's profit.'

'Which would be a fine thing.'

'Talk's a fine thing, too,' said Margrethe. 'You know the proverb? *"If wishes were horses, beggars would ride."* It's not too far from The Hague, so why don't you go to the counting-house of the East India Company and see what's offering? You could be there and back in a day.'

'You are right, Margrethe. I've an aunt at The Hague who would give us a bed for the night. What do you say, Abel?'

Abel looked at Jannetie, calmly counting the stitches in her knitting.

'Don't look at me, husband. You are the one who would have to take the berth they offered, if they offered anything.'

Abel felt himself at the cross-roads. If he ignored this chance, the subject might never come up again, and he would end his days shipping before the mast in the Baltic and North Sea trades. If he went to The Hague, if he joined the company, why the world was his oyster. Suddenly his mind was made up.

'We'll go to The Hague, Gerrit,' he said. 'And now what shall we drink to?'

Jannetie took the small taste of spirits he had offered her. 'I say we should drink to our decision.'

2

The Honest Trader

'GERRIT! By all that's holy, it's months since we met?'

'Nearer a year, you mean. How's the world treating you, Abel?'

'I can't complain. I miss the family life ashore, of course, but who doesn't?'

'Yes, I miss that too. Especially when a man has a son he's never seen.'

'My godson by proxy? How is he getting on?'

'He's got all his teeth, I'm told, and he can talk.'

'It's good that our wives are friends and can keep each other company. What about joining me in a jug of punch?'

'I'll not say no to that as long as it's more lime juice than arrack.'

They sat in the shade, grateful for the faint stir of air from the punkah overhead. After ordering their punch from the Ambonese steward, Abel turned to Gerrit. 'I hear you've got a command, Gerrit.'

'Yes, I took over the *Kameel* last month. That's why I asked for a weak punch. The last skipper dug his grave with the arrack flask.'

'Fever used to be the curse of these parts,' said Abel, 'but it seems it can be kept at bay with this new Peruvian bark. Now it's arrack that carries men off.'

'Arrack's a good servant to the seaman,' said Gerrit. The punch arrived, and he raised his cup to Abel 'Prost, shipmate! I don't know how we'd drink water six weeks in cask at sea without a little arrack to take the taste away. And here's to the skipper of the *Mocha*.'

'A fair wind and good profit, Gerrit. Here's to the skipper of the *Kameel*.'

'And to happy days in Amsterdam in 1636.'

'You can say that again. It will be three years come Christmas since we arrived here. Time certainly flies when one is occupied.' Abel recalled his thoughts while waiting for Jannetie in the Old Kirk, and the long discussions on time and duration with Gerrit in the *Weesp* on the passage out. 'Will you be signing a second contract?'

'Yes, if I can get a posting to Batavia. And later on, perhaps, a transfer to the merchant branch of the company.'

A stranger approached, and Gerrit half turned to speak to him. The deep voice under the trellised shade made a rich burr of sound, and the fragrance of tobacco mingled with the spicy cooking smells from the kitchen.

Even as a mate, thought Abel, a man could live like a prince in this country. Of course anyone in these waters risked a great deal, so it was only justice that he lived well ashore. Badly charted, laced with shifting coral and rocky islands, and with the threat of pirates, this was no place for the faint-hearted. The events of his last passage had proved that.

In the convoy with five other ships the *Mocha* had sailed from Ambon for Banda, north-about round the Isle of Ceram. This had been the idea of Frans Valck, commodore of the *Weesp*. It was the season of the easterly monsoon, and Valck thought that the longest way round might be the shortest way home.

The theory had been put to the test, and the commodore was proved right. But during the voyage they were attacked by seven catamarans, with crab-claw sails, and had lost five good top-men. The losses to the Dutch would have been greater, but their assailants were armed only with bamboo rocket-guns, and had been repulsed by cannon-shot and swivels firing case-shot of gravel and scrap-iron.

'That was one of my mates,' Gerrit said, 'wanting a

decision on something he could have thought out for himself.'

'The cares of office, Gerrit. That's why they pay you fifty guilders a month and a bonus each voyage.'

'That's right, Abel, but before I had command I'd never realized how hard a skipper worked.'

'Never mind. Amsterdam next year.'

'And pickled herring to give a thirst for good Dutch lager! Meanwhile that *rijstafel* from the kitchen smells good. What do you say?'

When his three-year contract expired, Abel joined the *Banda* for Amsterdam, working his way as chief mate. He arrived there in August 1637, surprising Jannetie in the kitchen, where she was making plum jam. They were almost shy with one another as she ladled the sweet-smelling stuff into jars and tied squares of parchment over the top.

Jannetie had changed very little in four years, but when Claesgen came running in to join them, Abel was amazed to see how much she had grown. After a few days together it was as if Abel had never been away.

They had sold their old house in Teerketel Lane, and with the money bought Gerrit Demmer's rented house in Palm Street. Gerrit and Margrethe had sailed to Ambon only three weeks before, and Abel was sorry to have missed his old shipmate; but, meanwhile, there was plenty to do.

The day after he arrived, he reported to the governor of the East India Company, who was a comfortable burgher in good broadcloth and starched linen.

'Mynheer Tasman! You arrived yesterday in the *Banda*?'

'Yes, Mynheer Brandt. We had a good passage of only five months.'

'And there will be a nice little bonus for you when the cargo is sold. I trust you found all well at home?'

'Very well, mynheer.'

'And do you wish to continue with the company?'

THE EAST INDIES

To illustrate the
Trading Activities of
The Netherlands East
India Company
about 1640

(Many thousands of
islands are not shown)

0 100 200 300 400 500
Miles

40°N

Korea

Japan Tokyo

Nagasaki

30°

China

Bonin Is.

Zeelandia

Formosa

20°

Cambodia

Philippines (Spanish)

30°

My Tho

Malaya

Sumatra

Borneo

0°

lembang

Celebes

New Guinea

Batavia

Ceram
Ambon

Java

Timor

10°S

New Holland

100°E   110°   120°   130°   140°E

Abel had his answer ready. He and Jannetie had talked at length about the future, and they felt that his prospects in the Far East would be better than in the bitter seas of the north.

'Yes, but only if I can be granted a passage for my family.'

'That can easily be arranged. We regard the first contract in the East as a trial period, because many who go out there do not want to return. It seems they find it difficult to accept the loneliness and responsibility of some of the stations. Now we have a good report on you, except for one small thing.'

'I can guess what that is, mynheer. I had trouble with my crew in the *Mocha*, and there was complaint against me at Ambon. I knew that one of the troublemakers, Adriaan Rijs, arrived here last June.'

'Yes, in the *Zandvoor*, and I heard his tale.'

'Would you tell me what he said, mynheer?'

'He claimed you stopped the issue of arrack to the crew for two months, and sold the spirit for your own profit.'

'The factor at Ambon investigated that charge, and his findings completely cleared me. Here is a copy of his report,' continued Abel, taking out a document and laying it in front of the governor.

Mynheer Brandt did not open it, but said, 'You tell me what happened.'

'Rijs, and two others, broke into the lazaret and broached a keg of arrack. The mate discovered this when the three were found to be drunk on watch.'

'That is a hanging matter, under company rules.'

'It is, indeed, but I did not hang them. They had wasted two months' arrack for three men, so I stopped their allowance for the same period. I did not have them flogged because I think it's a bad thing to flog Dutchmen in front of Asians, and half my crew were Javanese.' The governor nodded in agreement.

'Instead I ordered seven days' confinement on bread and

water. Later they also complained I had not given them any meat, oil or pickles for a month.'

The governor sighed. 'I had a feeling it would be like that, captain. Next time you have to punish a man for such a fault, make out a warrant of offence and punishment and have the guilty man sign it in front of witnesses. It saves much argument later.'

'Thank you for the advice, mynheer. I should have thought of that.'

'Well, one cannot think of everything. Now, we have a ship, the *Engel*, just launched and at present fitting out. I would like you to stand by her as she completes for sea, and sail her to Batavia in the spring.'

'Mynheer!' This was more than Abel had hoped for. 'Thank you very much.'

'You will be on half-pay until she sails.'

Abel was doubly pleased for this meant he would not have to live on his savings. 'And my family?' he asked.

Mynheer Brandt smiled. 'It is company policy that a captain's family sail with him in such circumstances, so you may take up quarters on board as soon as the ship is fit to live in.'

East Indiamen were particularly comfortable ships, because men often lived in them for years in the tropics. The Tasmans moved aboard in mid October, with tulips in pots of mould, Jannetie's linnet in a cage, and the cat, Blinkie. Jannetie soon adjusted to house-keeping on board, and found plenty of time to make hangings and cushions. By April 1638 the *Engel* was ready to sail.

'Take a long look at it, Jannetie,' said Abel as they stood together on deck watching the shore of the Texel fade astern. 'This is where our new life begins, and I do not care if we never see these parts again.'

'Nor do I Abel, truly, but I can't be like you. I've lived in Amsterdam all my life, and it's like leaving a part of me behind.' Jannetie turned her face from Abel's to hide the tears in her eyes.

The *Engel* was a new ship, so the run to the tip of Africa revealed the usual few faults. When they reached the Cape of Good Hope, Abel found a sandy beach which was marked on the charts, unloaded the ship, and beached her to renew the caulking near the keel. The work took nearly a month, and meanwhile they lived in tents ashore.

'This is such a different world, Abel,' Jannetie said on their first night ashore. 'Is it like this in the Indies?'

'Not very much,' Abel replied. 'Here the latitude corresponds to the south of Spain, but Batavia is very close to the equator so it is much warmer. You will not be complaining of a lack of sun.'

'Then I will get to like it, I'm sure.'

Claesgen came up with Blinkie in her arms. 'Don't people live in this country, father?'

'Not many, Claesgen. They belong to a race called the Hottentots, but this is my third time here, and I still haven't seen any. They are a shy people, I believe, and keep to themselves.'

'It is a wonder the company has not set up a factory here,' Jannetie said.

Abel shook his head. 'No trade, and no one to trade with. It's a poor country, for even the Hottentots are said to go naked. And while there are many deer-like creatures, there are also many lions and leopards.'

'So *that* is why you are having a fence built round the tents?'

'It is, and I'll set a watch, each man with a musket.'

Claesgen snuggled down beside the fire. 'You hear that, Blinkie? There are lions and leopards just outside, waiting to carry you off.'

Abel was particularly anxious to have the ship in sound condition because of the strong winds, the roaring forties, which blew in the southern hemisphere during the whole of the year.

With her leaks repaired, the *Engel* made her easting at the speed of a cantering horse, and during this period Abel was free to have talks with Jannetie.

'There must be a great deal of land still to discover in these parts, Abel. I never dreamt that there was so much salt water in the world.'

'In these latitudes a ship can sail for weeks without sighting shore, but there is land, if one goes far enough. For example, there's a place called New Holland, found by Willem Jansz and Jan Carstensz. It's reported that the natives there were as wretched as the Cape Hottentots.'

'Are the Dutch the only ones to have seen it?'

'Possibly, but I doubt it. There may have been Portuguese who kept quiet about it.'

'Why would they do that?'

'Trade secrets. Knowledge of currents and winds that the careful captain keeps to himself. Even now we are sailing a trade-secret course.'

Jannetie looked over the side. All she could see were albatrosses riding the air-waves astern, and above them an overcast sky with signs of a squall blowing up from the south. Abel smiled at her bewilderment.

'We are going to Batavia, which is not far from Portuguese Timor. The Portuguese reach their settlement by sailing round the Cape of Good Hope, and coasting up Africa as far as Mombasa. Then they beat across to Timor against the south-east trade winds, which was the way Vasco da Gama sailed to Goa. Now, we did not round the Cape at all, but sailed to the south of it and then turned east. As you've seen, Jannetie, the winds are steady and strong here every day from the west. We carry them as far as the longitude of Batavia, as near as we can judge, then turn north. Then we have steady winds, first on the starboard beam and then on the larboard. It's a rougher way, but about two months quicker.'

'And that is important, isn't it, Abel?'

'Important! It is indeed, for time is money in the Far-East trade.'

3

First Exploration

THERE was the usual crowd of merchants and clerks waiting to see the governor, but only one man there looked like a seaman. Abel took a chance on it and crossed the room to speak to him. 'Commodore Quast?'

'Captain Tasman! Please accept my apologies for superseding you in command of the *Engel.*'

'Please, commodore, there's no need to apologize. When I brought her from Amsterdam I knew the command was not permanent, and I am quite happy with my present ship.'

'The *Gracht*? Yes, she's a good vessel. But tell me what's the *Engel* like to sail?'

'Heavy on the helm, and inclined to hang in stays. I think she'd be better with the mainmast stepped two feet farther forward.'

'Maybe more sail on the bowsprit would help.'

Abel laughed. 'I've thought of that, but there's as much there as the spar will carry now. You'd lose the sprit in anything more than a fresh breeze.'

Matthew Quast chuckled, too, and Abel knew they would work together well. The time passed pleasantly in ship-talk until the crowd in the ante-room thinned and the governor was free to see them.

Anthony van Diemen had been Governor-General of the Dutch East India Company at Batavia for three years, and he looked a tired man. He was the director of a great trading combine, ruler of a multiracial empire, and shore admiral of a fleet sailing over half-known seas.

Keeping control of the fleet was van Diemen's difficult task. Dutch skippers resented interference, for the tradition of the sea-beggars was strong among them, and in Europe the sea-beggars were regarded as pirates. He looked warily at Abel and Quast as they entered the room, hoping they would agree to his proposition.

'Ah, mynheeren! What do you think of *Gracht* and *Engel* sailing together?'

'If that is the order, your excellency, we shall do so.'

'No formality in this room, gentlemen. We're just three captains discussing a voyage.' A servant poured a cup of punch for each of them, and van Diemen waved them into chairs. 'I think you have some idea of why I asked you to come here?'

'I have,' said the commodore. 'We are to look for the Gold and Silver Islands, the Tom Tiddler's ground that the Portuguese reported eastward of Japan.'

'You've heard of them, then?'

'Who hasn't?' Abel interjected. 'They talk about these wealthy islands even in Amsterdam.'

'And what do you think?'

'Who can say? A hundred years ago the Spaniards found much the same thing in Mexico.'

'These islands—the Rica de Oro and Rica de Plata—may well exist,' the commodore continued. 'There is rarely a shadow without a substance.'

'But they could well be in another direction from where we are told,' said Abel. 'One hears some strange stories from Portugal these days.'

'That might be so,' said van Diemen, 'but the directors at The Hague want us to investigate them, and I fully agree.'

'We'll be lucky if we make any profit out of this voyage.' The commodore shook his head.

'Don't be so gloomy, mynheer. If you find these islands, you might return ballasted with silver bars and eating off gold plate. Anyway, we are prepared to face a loss on this voyage because we make a great deal of money out of trade, and it is only right to spend some of it on exploration.'

'It's a good plan, but how would you suggest we go about it?' Abel asked van Diemen.

'By believing, in the first place, that the islands do exist. A Spanish captain, by the name of de Aguirre, says they were found when a Portuguese ship was blown by storm eight days east of Japan. The islanders, however, did not speak Japanese.'

'Well, that's a start. Did de Aguirre mention latitude?'

'Somewhere between 28° and 35° north, he said.'

'About two hundred leagues,' said the commodore, 'which is a fair stretch of ocean.'

'There are also many islands in that ocean, commodore. You've been out East long enough to know that.'

'I agree with Abel that they might lie in quite another direction. It's an old trick of seamen, giving wrong bearings to fool other men and other nations.'

'Well, if you find nothing, we might have a look along the north China coast. We know very little about those seas, either.'

Matthew Quast rubbed his chin. 'We can only try. But if we do our best and find nothing, there will be no bonus for us at the end of it.'

'I'll arrange all that, commodore. You'll be granted a bonus equal to that of a trading voyage.'

'That seems very fair,' Quast replied.

Abel, too, thought that the governor's offer was generous. Already his spirit began to stir with the challenge of finding new lands, and of pitting his strength against unfamiliar seas.

It was June 1639 when they sailed, and Abel was listed second in command in the Articles of the voyage.

The ships sailed north past Manila, coasting along Luzon

Island and rounding it to the north. Finding a good anchorage, they stopped to fill the water-casks on the largest of the Babuyan Islands.

They were collecting green coconuts when a boat appeared with four Filipinos and a Spanish priest. In Europe, Dutch and Spaniard could not have met on civil terms, but they were far from Europe now and both parties eagerly greeted each other.

The common language was French, which the commodore knew well, and which Abel could follow if simply expressed and slowly spoken. Padre Esteban had not heard of the Gold and Silver Islands, but he knew of others the Dutchmen were unfamiliar with. They were south of Japan, on the same longitude, and were uninhabited.

'These cannot be what we're looking for,' said Abel, 'for what about those rumours of gold cooking-pots?'

'We'll have to look at them just the same,' said the commodore. 'Who knows? The people might have all fled and left their kitchenware behind!'

After seven days' sail from the Babuyans they came across the first shoal, a fleck of silver surf on the blue ocean. *Engel*'s lookout saw it first, so it was pricked in on the charts and called Engel Shoal. Three days later they found two islands, well-wooded and lovely, but uninhabited. For the following three days they were never out of sight of reef or island, one showing up ahead as the other faded astern. They found good harbour on one of the islands, and dropped anchor. Abel and his mate were summoned to council in the *Engel*, where they found the commodore searching his charts and course books.

'Well, we've discovered something,' he said, 'for I cannot find these islands on any chart.'

'No name, and no inhabitants,' replied Abel. 'Yet they seem rich enough, judging by the height of the trees and the lush vegetation in the gullies.'

'Volcanic, very likely, Abel. Volcanic lands are always rich for some reason; look at Krakatoa! There was steam drifting from the land a while back, and several times I've caught a whiff of sulphur.'

'Maybe that's why there are no people. You wouldn't find me living by a volcano.'

'It doesn't seem to worry some. There are rice-paddies half-way up Krakatoa. Anyway, these are not the islands we came to find.'

'Not by leagues. I make the latitude 26° 50'. How does that agree with you?'

'Within two minutes. We'll stay and try to fix the longitude, working separately and averaging the results.'

'Yes, mynheer! And what would you say to felling some of those trees? They look very like cedars.'

Quast smiled at Abel. 'Cedarwood? Yes, that's always worth something.'

Back on *Gracht*, Abel set about fixing the longitude. Calculating latitude, north or south of the equator, had not been a problem since the time of Henry the Navigator, but longitude (the distance east or west of a given point) was quite a different matter. It could not be found by any method in a moving ship, but was fixed by sights, taken from the moon, on two or three clear nights ashore. So the longitude of the great ports of Europe was well known in relation to one another, and the seaman sailing from any one of them knew his point of departure. If he were sailing a long passage, he could check his whereabouts by known landfalls on the way, such as the Azores or the Cape of Good Hope; this would give him a new point of departure.

The usual way to reach a particular place was to sail to its latitude and try to keep to windward of it. From then on, a ship would sail downwind and look for landmarks until the destination was reached. By using compass, lead-line and the traverse-board some remarkable feats were accomplished. This method was called dead reckoning, and some captains, Abel among them, were so accurate it was said they could smell the land.

They spent three days on the island and found rosewood

and cedarwood, which meant that the voyage would not be entirely profitless. There were also wild melons, celery and pineapples, which were welcome additions to the food supply. Their calculations proved them to be on the same longitude as the east coast of Japan.

'We'll sail north until we sight Japan,' the commodore decided. 'That will give us a new point of departure, and a flying start.'

'If the Portuguese were blown eight days east by a storm,' said Abel, 'that would make the distance about three hundred and sixty leagues. I suggest we sail to 28° north, by dead reckoning, then begin looking.'

'With double lookouts in line abreast, heaving to at night and keeping contact with lanterns in the tops.'

'It'll be slow, but we shouldn't miss much that way.'

'And how long we continue looking depends on the water supply. When we get down to fourteen days on half-rations, we had better turn back.'

It took twenty days to run their easting down. After the first five the sailing was easy, for they moved into a region of steady westerly winds, blowing at about nine knots.

There was a growth of weed on the bottom of both ships, so stagings were rigged over the sides and the hands set to with breaming-irons to get rid of as much as possible. Although they could only reach about a yard beneath the waterline, there was a noticeable improvement in speed.

So they reached a point where their real search was to begin, and the officers gathered to discuss details.

'I thought of a sweep-search,' said the commodore. 'Two days east, half a day north, then three days west, and repeat, using the pinnaces to connect the ships and to extend the line.'

Abel nodded in agreement. Ship, pinnace, pinnace, ship; these could search a band of ocean three-quarters of a degree of latitude. Five such sweeps, and if the Gold and Silver Islands were where de Aguirre said they were, then they must surely find them. 'That will be exhausting work for the pinnace-crews if they have to use the oars,' he said.

'We'll heave to at night. The ships will close up to within sight of one another, and the pinnaces change crews during the silent hours.'

'That's a good solution. If they left the ships during the first watch, the men could be back on station by daybreak.'

It was arduous work as eyes strained ahead to catch the loom of land that never appeared and watch was kept for the white flash of the pinnace sail. It was high summer, with cloudless skies day after day and never a drop of rain. Such weather was good for the search, but bad for the water supply. What was left in the casks grew foul with green slime, so that straining it through charcoal failed to sweeten it. Even when made into punch, with lime juice and arrack, it was barely drinkable.

On the evening of the sixth sweep, Matthew Quast flew the signal for a council, and Abel rowed across from the *Gracht*. He looked back, thinking what a picturesque sight his ship was, lying hove-to, the reflection of lanterns glowing in the water.

'How's the health on the *Gracht*, Abel?' was the commodore's greeting.

'Two men have died and others are sickening—all Javanese.'

'Scurvy, do you think?'

'It could be. Scurvy often affects each man differently.'

'That's true. Five of my men have died, and I'm sure it's scurvy. But I've neither limes nor onions left'—both these were well known to prevent scurvy—'and the water's almost too foul to drink.'

'Mine's no better, but I've some onions left so I'll send half of them across.'

'Thanks, Abel. Let's go back while we can, and at least we can mark on the charts a position where the Gold and Silver Islands are not!'

'I agree, commodore. There's no point in becoming the Flying Dutchmen of the Pacific, for ever sailing east and west, playing dice with the Devil.'

They made one more sweep, reaching to 32°54' north before turning east and beating to Formosa. When they dropped anchor off the company's post at Zeelandia, at the end of November 1639, Quast and Tasman were weary men.

'Ah, Captain Tasman, you have had a good trip from Formosa, I hope.' It was the end of February 1640. Abel had spent Christmas on Formosa, half wishing he were with Jannetie, and half wishing they had been able to go on looking for the Gold and Silver Islands. They might still exist somewhere, but the ocean was so vast and their ships were so small.

'Not bad, mynheer, not bad. No doubt the commodore has told you of our losses at sea?'

'Yes, a sad toll and a heavy price to pay for not much of a result.'

'We may not have found the Gold and Silver Islands, but the islands south of Japan have good water and fruit, to say nothing of the rosewood and cedarwood. I'd call that some result, mynheer.'

'I agree that a peaceful watering-place is worth a great deal in those seas. But your main quest, what of that?'

'I was thinking it over in Formosa. The latitude is about right, though the distance from Japan is wrong. But, governor, you know how stories become distorted. Anyway, it's all in the journal.' Abel pointed to the canvas-bound log-books on the table between them. 'Courses, landfalls, weather and health: all written down, with nothing left out.'

'And you, like Commodore Quast, are sure there are no islands?'

'Not where we looked, nor anywhere within two days' sail of there.'

'Why do you say two days' sail?'

'Because we saw no birds. Only one bird I know of keeps to the sea without returning to sleep on shore—the albatross of the roaring forties. But I've never seen one north of the Line.'

'You are observant, captain. If you were to go and look again for these islands, where would you begin?'

'Farther to the north and farther east. Also I would begin earlier in the year. Why, do you want us to go again?'

'Not just yet, captain, not just yet. As I said before, trade must pay for discovery, and the coffers are empty for this year. Now, the *Oostcappel* is lying at Onrust, and I want you to commission her for a voyage to Japan. Go over and have a look at her, then let me know when you can sail.'

Abel Tasman was worth watching, thought the governor, opening one of the logbooks the captain had left behind. The company had plenty of skilled seamen, some of whom were good traders, but few were fine navigators capable of making a course-book or plotting a chart as Tasman could. And what's more he had run a happy ship on a well-nigh profitless voyage. Yes, he would follow this man's career with interest.

4
Ambassador-at-Large

'THIS voyage will be different from any you have sailed before—neither exploration nor trade.'

'I'm afraid I don't understand, mynheer.'

'You'll be an armed ambassador, commodore, with trade, as it offers, on the side.'

Commodore! Abel knew he would have five ships under his command, but this was the first time Governor van Diemen had given him his title. He flushed a little, but said calmly, 'We are always armed in these waters.'

'Very sensibly, in case you are attacked by pirates. But this time we may be faced with open war.'

'The Spaniards of the Philippines, or the Portuguese from Goa?'

'Neither, it's the Japanese. I hope we can keep the peace, but we must be prepared.'

'And I was hoping to take my wife with me on this voyage.'

'Sorry, commodore. Almost any other voyage, but not this one.'

'Why war with the Japanese after we gave help to the shogun when his subjects rebelled at Hara, three years ago?'

'I don't understand it, either,' said van Diemen dryly. 'Of the peoples in this part of the world, I'm not sure the Japanese aren't the most difficult to comprehend. Even their religions seem to be the exact opposite to Christianity.'

'But didn't the Jesuits make Christian converts?'

'Yes, they did. But the shogun saw them as a threat to

the god-emperor and, therefore, to his government. Suddenly he slaughtered the lot. There were thirty-five thousand Japanese killed, I believe.'

Abel's expression was grim. Over the last sixty years there had been more than that number of Dutch killed in the name of religion in the United Provinces of the Netherlands. 'Religious wars have been going on for a long time,' he said.

'Yes. But the shogun did not kill the rebels for being Christians; he killed them for not paying taxes.'

'That's no reason for killing people.'

'The taxes were high, up to seventy per cent. But ten per cent of something would have been better than seventy per cent of nothing.'

The governor handed Abel a parchment. 'Here are the instructions written down by the council, but I can give you the gist of them. Go to Formosa, and get the latest news; then to Japan, where you will put yourself under the orders of the council at Firando—so long as it does not involve too much hazard to ships or crews.'

'I'm glad that's in writing, about risking the ships.'

'Yes, I insisted on that. Our trade with Japan is valuable and it's worth a little risk to retain it.'

'As well as being a slap in the face for the Portuguese.'

'Yes, and the English. They've got the Great Mogul in their pockets, so let's do what we can to keep on terms with the shogun.'

'I'll bear that in mind, mynheer.'

'I'm sure of that. You showed yourself as a good navigator in your last voyage, and you can prove you are an equally good ambassador.'

Abel had plenty of time for thinking as the *Oostcappel* sailed north. Six years earlier he had arrived in the East, a seaman before the mast on his first contract. Who would have thought then that he would be sailing in command of a fleet, on a mission that might mean the difference between peace and war?

It felt odd not to be involved with the daily running of the ships, but he was getting used to it when the flotilla ran into Zeelandia harbour and he was greeted, for the first time, with a commodore's salute of seven guns. He was not really surprised to find the factor was the same Mynheer Brandt he had seen two years before in Amsterdam.

'Commodore Tasman! Let me see, it was in Amsterdam we met, was it not?'

'Two years ago, mynheer. I have mail for you from the governor in Batavia.'

A steward served punch while the factor read his mail. When he had finished, he looked at Abel. 'I see you are to sail for Firando, our factory in Japan. I only hope it's still there when you arrive.'

'Things are as bad as that, are they?'

'In Japan they could not be much worse. If we don't play our cards carefully, we will be forced from the country, just like the Portuguese.'

'That's exactly what Governor van Diemen is afraid of.'

'We all are. Trade with Japan has never been easy, but lately it's been almost impossible.'

'Because of the Jesuits?'

'Only partly. The present unrest has little to do with either us or the Portuguese. It's a dispute between the Japanese peasant, who is a hard-working little man, and his daimio, or baron. The country is split up into provinces, and each province is ruled by a daimio. So, in effect, it's the daimios who really rule Japan.'

'But what about the shogun? Isn't he the king?'

'It's more complicated than that, but I will try and explain. The daimio collects as much tax as he thinks the province can pay. Some of this he hands over to the shogun, the prince who runs the central government, but most of it he keeps for himself. So you see the shogun is not the king, but a sort of chief minister, whose powers pass down from father to son. The king of Japan is called the mikado.'

'So the mikado gives orders to the shogun?'

'No. Nor is it the other way round. The mikado is descended, they say, from the Japanese sun-god. He lives in seclusion, and the people never see him.'

Abel laughed. 'If all goes well, the shogun takes the credit, and if things are bad, the mikado takes the blame! Is that it?'

'No, for as well as being descended from a god, the mikado *is* a god. So he can do no wrong. When trouble broke out in Kyushu province it was blamed on the Christians, and indirectly on the Portuguese because they had made the converts.'

'Ah! You are right, mynheer, it is very difficult.'

'Now, this might not sound very honest, but business is business. Because we are opposed to the Portuguese, it suited our interests to aid the daimio in Kyushu against the rebels. So we are in his favour and the Portuguese are not, since they favoured his enemies.'

'Confidentially, I do too. But I can see that for the company's sake we must stay in favour with the daimio and the shogun.'

'Yes, strive to keep the peace with the Japanese. Speak to them fairly, but keep your powder dry!'

The factor at Firando was Francis de Witt, a man of Abel's age who had been in the Indies since his youth, and consequently knew a great deal about Asian people.

'You are as welcome as tulips in springtime,' he said. 'A few well-armed ships might make all the difference as to whether we go or stay in Japan. You know the shogun has expelled the Portuguese?'

'Mynheer Brandt in Formosa told me there was trouble between them.'

'Well, they've sent them packing, and they could well do the same to us. The Japanese are forbidden to trade direct with the company. There's a law that if they take any Portuguese ship, they are to burn it, hull and cargo, and behead the crew.'

'They've really got it in for the Portuguese!'

'Commodore, they don't like any Europeans. Every port, except Nagasaki, is closed to foreign ships, and we are the only people allowed there. Sometimes I'm afraid to shake my head, it feels so loose on my shoulders!' He paced the room; his thoughts would not let him stand still. 'You are protestant, commodore?'

'Yes, I'm from Groningen, well above the rivers.'

'H'mmm, that might help.'

'In what way, mynheer?'

'We've told the shogun we are not the same religion as the Portuguese, which I admit is only a half-truth. Now he has said that all who are his friends—one might as well be friends with a Sumatran tiger!—must perform the ceremony of efumi.'

'Efumi? What is that?'

'It means one has to trample on the pictures of our Lord which once hung in Portuguese churches.'

'Oh, no!' Abel was horrified.

'I see you feel the same as I did—nauseated. But I did it. And not for the sake of the company or trade, but for Dutch lives. If you are asked to do efumi, I advise you to do so.'

Abel said nothing.

'Commodore! Please?'

'All right. I'll do it if I have to.'

Francis de Witt wiped his forehead. 'It's dreadful, I know, but I'm glad you've agreed. Incidentally, we've got a quorum on the Japanese council at present. Will you agree to being a member while you stay here? At the usual fee, of course.'

The next four months were anxious ones for the Dutch. Negotiations with the daimio were difficult: as soon as one objection was overcome, another was raised. Finally it was agreed that the Dutch should leave the comfortable factory at Firando and move to Nagasaki.

'Well, we still have a toehold,' said de Witt. 'But only just. It's going to be no joke living on Deshima.'

'What is Deshima?' asked one of the captains.

'It's the old Portuguese factory on an island in the harbour, built up by dumping garbage. It's infested with rats, and the cellars flood at high tides.'

'Look on the bright side,' said Abel. 'Some good Dutch tomcats will see to the vermin, and if there's one thing we Dutch can do, it's build dykes to keep out the sea.'

Four days after Christmas, Abel left Nagasaki and sailed for My Tho, a port on the Mekong River. It was a relief to be away from Japan and among the gentle Cambodians, who were pleasant to deal with. He spent three months trading there. It was not until March 1641 that the flotilla left, deep-laden with spices, silks and lacquer-ware. During his stay Abel had learnt something of the Cambodian language, and on the way home he learnt something of the Laotian tongue, because seven merchants took passage with him in order to discuss matters of trade with the governor in Batavia.

After five weeks at home the *Oostcappel* sailed again, going first to My Tho with the Laotian merchants, and from there under orders to Japan. At My Tho, Abel took on a lading of hardwood and cleared for Deshima on 7th June. Before he left, the factor had a word with him.

'You know the Japanese have put a ban on all Portuguese ships, commodore?'

'That's common knowledge from here to Timor, mynheer. Why are you asking?'

'One day's sail from the Mekong you will meet three Cambodian junks. You will attack them, capture the largest, and bring it back to My Tho. You will almost capture the second largest, but it will escape. The smallest you will not attack, and it will escape unmolested.'

Abel knew it was a plot. 'And why am I to play the pirate, mynheer?'

'The largest junk is loaded with Portuguese goods. They are ours really, obtained by honest trade.'

'Then why the pretence of capturing them?'

'To deceive the Japanese. We shall see to it they hear of the capture, and spies will certainly tell them of the two which escaped. They may blame you for that, and even claim compensation from the company for your negligence. The company might even pay what they ask, holding you at fault.'

Abel was an even-tempered man, but his patience was being tried. 'Now see here—'

'Peace, friend, it will not be held against you.'

'I should hope not. But what's the object?'

'It was the only way we could think of landing some Cambodian friends in Japan without arousing suspicion. The Japanese will not hear about the capture until the Cambodians have been landed, and the daimio's troops will be so busy looking for Portuguese they'll never notice a few Cambodians. They look very like the Japanese.'

'And?'

'The Japanese have no friends outside Japan, but there are still some Japanese Christians who escaped the shogun's headsmen. The Cambodians are also Christians, which means we shall have friends inside the enemy camp.'

5

Chances of Trade

'No doubt about it,' the governor said, putting down his tankard. 'We've done well out here in the past forty years. But if the Japanese and Chinese allied, or if either of them were to join with the pirate rajahs in Sumatra, that would cook the company's goose, and there'd be a lot of Dutch throats slit into the bargain.'

It was January 1642, and Abel and a company mapmaker, Francis Visscher, were dining with the governor. Their wives had withdrawn into the parlour for coffee, and their voices could be heard coming faintly through the carved teak door into the dining-room, where the men sat over their wine. The madeira went round again, and Abel topped up his glass.

'Asians cannot agree any better than Europeans,' he said, 'and we may thank God for it. By the way, did they accept at the shogun's court that it was my fault that the Cambodian junks escaped?'

'Oh, yes, you'll see on your account that you've been fined two months' pay and reprimanded, but don't take any notice. There's no mention of it on your documents here, and we made up the fine by increasing your pay and back-dating the increase. But—'

'But what, mynheer?'

'It puts you out of court as far as Japan or Cambodia is concerned, at least until there's a change of shogun. The present one thinks you've been sent back to the provinces in disgrace, and he must go on thinking that.'

'I'm not worried, as long as you know the truth. I can

do with a spell after the past year?'

'In your last journal you mentioned you'd been dismasted off Formosa. I'd like to hear about that. I've had most things happen to me at sea, but I've never been dismasted.'

Abel laughed as he lit his pipe. 'You've not missed much, as the Flemings say, eh, Francis.'

He sat for a moment looking round the quiet room—at the attentive servants waiting for orders, the polished wood and the silver lamps. Then he began. 'We were struck four days out of Formosa,' he said, 'and we didn't even have time to get the sails off her. We tried to heave to, but couldn't with the sail up. After the foot-ropes parted and we lost two men, we couldn't heave to at all.'

'I take it your canvas held?'

'Only too well. It was new stuff, fresh from Haarlem. Just after we got the remaining men down from aloft, we were taken aback, and the forestay parted.'

Abel could still remember it, a split-second disaster that seemed to last for hours. There was a noise as loud as a cannon-shot and the mast slowly folded like the blade of a clasp-knife being closed.

'What happened to the main and mizen?'

'The main followed the fore, but the mizen lasted long enough to blow us head to wind. There were times when I thought we would roll over.'

'Did you see anything of this from *Zeeloewe*, mynheer?'

'Nothing at all,' replied Francis. 'We were having our own troubles.'

'To be sure! Please go on, commodore.'

'There's not much more to tell. We had to cut the wreckage clear, or the pounding of the masts would have driven our sides in. We lost another man doing this, dragged overboard in the bight of a rope.'

'It's not a situation I'd like to be in.'

'But we did have one bit of luck. When the mizen went, it went over the stern and made a very good sea-anchor. I think it was that which saved us.'

'We saw the last of your mizen two days later when the weather cleared,' Francis said. 'You were lucky it held until then.'

'We were both lucky that your sails blew out.'

'Why, commodore?' asked the governor.

'By losing sail we saved our spars. It's easier to bend new sail than rig new masts,' said Francis.

'*Zeeloewe* salvaged our mizen mast and took us in tow,' said Abel, 'but until then—goodness, how we rolled! I've not been so sick since I was a lad in the herring smacks on the Dogger Bank.'

'And after all this you contrived a jury-rig and got back to Formosa?'

'It's amazing what you can do if your life depends on it, mynheer. That waterfront in Zeelandia was the finest sight I ever saw in my life!'

After these voyages Abel had four months at home in Batavia. Jannetie was now thirty and had developed a matronly figure which made her look older than she was. Her only regret was that she had never borne a child, but it was a consolation to her that Claesgen, now twelve, could not remember any other mother. Abel had no wish for more children, and he didn't want to lose Jannetie as he had lost Claesgie. During their periods together they were a happy little family in their home down by the customs house.

The *Oostcappel* went to Onrust for a refit, and Abel was appointed to the prize court to judge the value of some captured Portuguese ships. For this duty he drew his captain's pay and an extra fee for being employed ashore, so he was not out of pocket through the long spell away from sea.

The business of the prize court was finished, and he was walking in the compound one morning when the governor's palanquin stopped at the gate.

'Well, good morning, your excellency. You do not come to visit us often enough.'

'There are too many calls on my time, commodore. They say a man in public office becomes a piece of public property, you know.'

'We were about to have a pot of coffee, mynheer,' said Jannetie, curtsying. 'Would you join us?'

'With all the will in the world.'

Jannetie ordered the coffee, and they made small-talk until it was served and the steward had left.

The governor sipped heartily and said, 'As you've probably guessed, I did not come to drink coffee and exchange gossip. I want you to make a voyage to Palembang.'

'Well, that should not take long. It's practically next door.'

'Commodore, this voyage will be no test of your skill as a seaman. It is more a matter of delicacy.'

'A diplomatic voyage, not a matter of fighting?'

'If it comes to fighting, then the mission will probably fail.'

'Then again I cannot go!' exclaimed Jannetie. 'And I was looking forward to being with my husband on his next voyage.'

The governor considered for a moment. 'And why not? Go, by all means, Mevrouw Tasman. This is a diplomatic voyage, and perhaps the best way of ensuring a peaceful outcome is by having a lady on board.'

'All I know of Palembang is that there are pirate rajahs in those parts,' said Abel. 'What is it that you want us to do?'

Palembang lies twenty-two leagues inland, at the point where the Musi River forks into arms round a swampy delta. *Ruttém* and her consorts, *Reebok* and *Moewe*, took three days to reach it after crossing the bar at the river-mouth.

Abel flew his pennant in the *Ruttém*, a sailing vessel of one hundred tonnes, rigged as a three-masted ship. The other ships were smaller, but all were broad-beamed and hard-bilged, giving them an almost flat bottom. They were good ships for exploring swampy deltas and for sitting on the mud at low tide.

They went up the river on the flowing tide, anchoring and taking the mud as it ebbed. Despite the intense heat and the swarms of insects, Jannetie was fascinated by the journey. There was a variety of things to see, for the river was both dwelling-place and thoroughfare for the Sumatrans.

During the forenoon of the fourth day they came to Palembang. With the crew at the sweeps, they drifted up the last reach towards the township, and Abel summoned his officers for a council.

'In the first place,' he said, 'we are on a mission of guile rather than force. However, rig the boarding-nets at nightfall and see that the swivels are loaded. But, if we have to fight, we will have failed in our mission. The object of our exercise is to capture a Chinese merchant prince, called Eng Po Tang. He pretends to be our friend, but we know he is trying to combine a number of rajahs against the company. We wish him no harm, but the governor wants to speak to him. If we can take him from here in a way that will make him a laughing-stock, so much the better.'

'I've heard of Eng Po Tang,' said Henrik Gerritsen, one of the mates. 'He never stirs from his house without a guard. But if you can make a fool of him, he will lose face with the rajahs.'

'That's what we hope to do. The ships will anchor by the stern, so that we can get away quickly if we have to. No shore-leave except on my orders, and keep the bumboats at a distance. Remember, not a word of this to the men.'

Most of the building in Palembang was attap, a combination of bamboo and palm-thatch. Buffaloes wallowed in mud-holes in the unpaved streets, and the mixture of smells included sewage, marigolds and spice. But Abel was no stranger to stench and squalor and scarcely gave the place a second look as he walked towards the company godowns.

The factory had a solid stone wall round it, enclosing an area of unburnt-brick buildings with thatched roofs. The factor was Peter Grobelaar, a stoutly built man whose face was yellowed with fever. When Abel found him, he was in his counting-house sitting under the punkah.

'Good morning, commodore. I take it you're from the *Ruttém*? What have you got for me?'

Abel handed over a copy of his manifest, and the factor scanned it quickly. 'Delft, cloth, cutlery and ironware—I can do good trade with these.' He handed the manifest to a comprador saying, 'See that lighters are sent out to the ships unless—' and he turned to Abel—'you'd rather I arrange a berth for you alongside?'

'No, I'd rather stay out in the stream,' Abel replied. He waited until the comprador was out of earshot and said, 'Is there a place where we could speak without being overheard?'

'Ah, I wondered about your three ships.' Then, in a louder voice, 'I take a cup of punch about this time, commodore, under the awning on the watch-tower. There's a breeze up there, and I can keep an eye on what is going on. Will you join me?'

'With pleasure. It's a thirsty walk from the riverfront.'

When they were settled in long rattan chairs on the watch-tower the factor asked, 'Now, why are you really here, commodore?'

'Governor van Diemen wishes to speak with Eng Po Tang.'

'You'll never get him to go to Batavia.'

'My orders are to see that he does, by force if need be.'

'That's a tall order, commodore. Do you know why he is here?'

'I have heard that he is trying to combine the rajahs against the company.'

'Well, that's one reason, but the other is that he is out

to buy cannon. You've been given a difficult task, commodore.'

Abel grinned. 'The day I'm asked to do an easy one, I will die of shock. This is no worse than other tasks I've been set.'

'And what are your plans?'

'I haven't any, as yet. And before I make one, I need to know more about Eng Po Tang.'

'Maybe I can help. I'm giving a dinner party tomorrow afternoon, and he will be there. He's a great one for his food, and my cook is one of the best in the city. You must come too.'

'Excellent, mynheer, excellent! Will it offend local custom if I bring my wife?'

'You brought your wife on such a mission? Was that wise?'

'We thought it would avoid suspicion.'

'Bring her, by all means. Mevrouw Grobelaar will be pleased to see a new face.'

The dinner party was a great success, and the guests were still toying with sweetmeats and strong waters long after sunset. Eng Po Tang did not look a dangerous man. He was very fat, and to show that he did no work with his hands, his fingernails were long and protected by lacquer sheathes which made a dry clicking noise as he gestured. One of his attendants was a boy whose sole duty was to feed his master with a pair of carved ivory chopsticks.

Since he was the chief guest, the meal could not end until he had finished. At last Eng Po Tang belched and said, 'An excellent repast, mynheer! May the heavenly ones requite you tenfold.'

'A cup of cordial, highness?' asked the factor. 'I have one blended with rare herbs, which is used in our country to settle the stomach.'

'Then pour me some, host!' He raised his cup to Jannetie

in the European style. 'To your great beauty, my lady.'

Jannetie was no great beauty, and she knew it. But she bowed to the Chinese and drank from her own cup in reply.

'Our foreign wines give you pleasure, highness?' asked Abel.

'They do, commodore. Wines are the best goods you bring us from the West.'

'I doubt if you have tasted the finest of them,' Abel said, the beginning of a plan forming in his mind. 'The ones we have drunk today are—and Mynheer Grobelaar will excuse me for saying so—for young men only.'

'And what are the wines that are fit for men of riper years, commodore?'

'Well, there is usquebaugh from Scotland, or French *eau-de-vei*, or Swedish aquavit, but these should be drunk either in their native land or on the ship that carries them. If they are brought ashore, their essence is lost.'

'I have not heard that. Though I can see it makes good sense.'

'It is very true, highness,' said the factor. He turned to Abel. 'I'll guarantee you have some of the best liquor on board, commodore?'

'Indeed, I have. There's a keg of aquavit that has crossed the Line four times!'

Like all successful traders, the factor could act. His eyes shone, and his tongue flickered over his lips. 'I trust you will invite me aboard so I can taste this, commodore? H'mmm, four times across the Line.'

'Come on board tomorrow, and I'll prove that you have never tasted anything better.'

'Tuan bezar,' said Eng Po Tang, 'I too would like to taste this divine spirit.'

'Certainly!' said Abel, feigning naïvety. 'You'll be very welcome on board.' He turned to the factor. 'If I could borrow your cook, I might attempt to return your hospitality.'

'An excellent thought, commodore. We'll drink another

one to that.'

The Chinese plucked at Abel's sleeve with his insect-like hands. 'I have discussed the matter of cannon with your factor,' he said, 'but, alas, with no result. Maybe, if I were to arrive before the other guests, we could speak a little business?'

'Don't let Mynheer Grobelaar hear you,' Abel said in a loud whisper. 'The company does not deal in arms. But that does not mean we cannot come to an arrangement—one gentleman to another.'

'So far, so good,' said Peter Grobelaar the next morning. He had brought his cook and assistant out to the *Ruttém*, and they were now busy preparing for the feast. 'Here's the poppy juice to dope the bodyguard.'

Abel took the flask carefully. 'I've never used this before. How much should be put in the punch?'

'About half a flask to the gallon.'

'And how do I give it to the Chinese without knocking out my own crew?'

'Nothing simpler! The doped punch will be mixed in a yellow pitcher, since yellow's a lucky colour among the Chinese. The plain lime juice for the crew will be in a white jug, and the Chinese won't touch that.'

'Ah, I see. White is their colour of mourning—the colour of death. I won't, of course, dope Eng Po Tang.'

'He wouldn't put up a fight. He'll be much too afraid of breaking his fingernails.'

It was mid afternoon, and, as arranged, the Chinese arrived early. The tantalizing smell of cooking drifted from forward, while the guests sat aft in a circle chattering and smoking long bamboo pipes.

'They are indeed beautiful guns, tuan bezar,' said Eng Po Tang.

The guns Eng Po Tang was referring to were bronze pieces captured in the Spanish Wars and bearing the arms of Philip of Spain on the apron. They had been cleaned that morning, and glistened in the afternoon sun. But they had been rebored more than once, and while they would make a fine show flanking the gateway to a rajah's palace, they would be a danger to the gunner if fired with a full charge.

Eng Po Tang's eyes gleamed. 'They are so beautiful that I feel my ill-stocked godowns do not hold sufficient goods to trade for them.'

'Between friends there is no need to haggle,' said Abel, 'but we can talk of that some other time. Let us drink *sherberts* under the awning until my other guests arrive.'

Eng Po Tang commended the egg-flower soup, praised the sweet-and-sour fish, and was ecstatic about the crisp-skin duck. Dish after dish came to the guest on the poop, and the remains went forward to the bodyguard on the hatchtop. Abel saw the yellow pitcher passing freely from hand to hand, and heard the voices become more and more slurred.

Tonight Eng Po Tang, seated on a cushion, was attended by two boys. One tasted every dish in case of poison, and the other was the boy with the chopsticks who fed him. The bodyguard, leaning on his sword behind the merchant, looked unhappy, doubtless wondering if there would be anything left when it came to his turn to eat and drink. Abel and the factor tried to appear relaxed, despite their mood of anticipation. They were, in fact, waiting for silence. Gradually the laughter and talk forward faded and died, and it was obvious that the poppy juice was doing its work.

Abel nodded to the women, who rose and went quietly below. No one noticed the serang and the two seamen who slipped into a dinghy and sculled round the stern. Coming aboard by the anchor cable, they stole forward round the hatch. The bodyguard only realized that something was wrong when a silk scarf looped round his throat, and stopped his breathing. His hands clawed at the scarf, and his sword dropped to the deck.

'Bind him, but do not kill!' Abel ordered. Forward, the rest of the bodyguards were bound, hand and foot, and laid in a neat row. 'Take the boys and Eng Po Tang and bind them, too.'

The Chinese made a move towards the bodyguard's dropped sword, but the sight of two long wheel-lock pistols in Abel's hands made him think better of it. When he was secured, the factor called to his wife and handed her over the side into his waiting boat.

'You'll be wanting to get away, no doubt,' he said to Abel, 'and I'll not detain you. By God, but there'll be some laughter round Palembang when this gets out!'

Eng Po Tang almost burst with rage at the thought of being outwitted and bound by a foreign devil.

'Release me! Or, by the Heavenly Ones, every person in the ship will die the death of the thousand cuts!'

'I doubt that,' said Abel, feeling the breeze as the ship gathered way with the crew at the sweeps. He hauled down a rope ready rove at the mizen-yard and fitted a noose round the merchant's neck. 'And if we do, you will not see it. Up you go at the first sign of attack, and I'll cut off your pigtail for good measure first!' He laughed at the look of terror on Eng Po Tang's face. 'But have no fear, I was asked to take you alive, if possible. The governor at Batavia does not like your friends, the rajahs, and would like to have a talk with you.'

New Lands: 1642-1643

1

Beyond all Charting

IT was July 1642 and Anthony van Diemen and his wife were entertaining four guests at the coolness of Bogor in the hills. They were Abel Tasman, Francis Visscher, and their wives.

To reach Bogor from Batavia was a two-day journey by riverboat, followed by a half-day trip by mule or litter through jungled hill-slopes. Abel wondered what was on the governor's mind, for van Diemen was a canny man who did nothing without a reason.

On the second day of their visit the governor called them into his study, for even at Bogor a courier came daily with a satchel of documents from the capital. In the centre of the room stood a teakwood table littered with charts. Abel knew some of them, and on top lay Gerritz's chart of a group of islands he had named the South Land.

The governor filled his pipe and pushed the tobacco jar across. 'Sit down, gentlemen. No doubt you are wondering why I asked you to Bogor?'

'Well, we guessed it was not entirely for the pleasure of our company.'

'Oh, I enjoy that—and I like this place myself. But it gives me a chance to talk things over without interruption, which is impossible down in the city. Now there's a voyage I've long had in mind.'

'To the South Land, no doubt,' Abel said dryly.

'Ah, you noticed the charts? Yes, that was the project I thought of.'

'Well, you have all the charts in existence on the subject,' said Visscher, who was an expert on charts, 'though some of them are not very detailed.'

'I agree,' said van Diemen, settling in his chair. 'But I think it is also agreed that a great landmass must lie between here and the South Pole. We, as well as the Portuguese and the Spaniards, have all seen parts of it.'

'True enough,' said Abel, 'half a score of seamen have sighted unknown land to the south.'

'Yes, many have seen something, sometimes different things in the same places. Hessel Gerritz, of course, was not a seaman, but he collected all the different sightings and placed them on one chart.'

By this time they were standing round the chart table. 'Gerritz doesn't appear to accept the fact that de Torres reported a strait cutting through the middle of New Guinea.'

'Neither would I until I saw it,' said Francis. 'Anyone who believed a Spanish or Portuguese chart would believe that the moon was made of cheese!'

'They were the greatest seamen in the world in the days of Cortez and Pizarro.'

'But that's more than a hundred years ago.'

'Well, we did not come here to talk about the short-comings of the Spanish,' said the governor. 'And as to Torres's strait—well, it might be one of you who will prove it one way or the other.'

'I know nothing of those parts.' Abel sounded apprehensive.

'Nor I, except from the charts,' said Visscher. 'What was it you had in mind, mynheer?'

'Two things,' said van Diemen. 'To find possible fresh markets for the company, and to increase our knowledge of the world.'

Abel riffled through the charts on the table. 'From what I see set down on these charts the South Land seems to be mostly desert. There is little profit in deserts.'

The governor smiled. 'Much of the coast of Africa is desert. Yet there are great cities there, rich in trade. There may be cities in this South Land, too, just waiting to be found.'

'Some voyagers have reported seeing naked savages, governor. So it seems unlikely there would be cities.'

'Yes, but perhaps the west coast of New Holland can be compared with the African south-west in the same latitude, which is so barren it is called the Skeleton Coast.'

'Because it is also littered with wrecks,' said Francis. 'They say that no ship caught there on a lee shore ever wins clear.'

'That may well be true. Africa and South America both have south-west coasts hostile to ships.'

Abel began to see the drift of van Diemen's argument, and felt a prickle of interest. 'So?' he said.

'It might be the same with the South Land. It's been sighted half a dozen times over a distance of five hundred leagues, and what has been seen? A few bare-breeched savages who don't even build huts, a few dried-up creeks but no rivers, and, except in the extreme south, no trees. Another Skeleton Coast, in fact.'

'I think I see,' said Francis Visscher. 'You think—'

'I think there may be something elsewhere. We know nothing, for instance, about this land's south or east coast—not even where it lies.'

'You are thinking of Africa again?' said Abel. 'The Portuguese do a good trade with the cities of Zanzibar and Mombasa on the east coast.'

'I was also thinking of the east coast of South America. Rio de Janeiro and Buenos Aires are flourishing cities, though they were founded not long ago. Who knows what the discoverers of the east coast of the South Land may find!'

'Look what the Spaniards found in Mexico, and there were no cities on the coast,' said Visscher.

'Yes, inland there was fabulous wealth. And there might be as many good things to be found when we reach the east or south coasts of this South Land.'

Abel called to mind the men who had reported sighting the South Land. Most had been ordinary captains driven off-course, and their discoveries had been by chance. 'If I were to set out on this ploy,' he said, 'I should want two ships, at least. Who's going to pay for them?'

The governor laughed. 'Part of the cost will be borne by Eng Po Tang,' he said, 'who—ah—agreed to subscribe to the cost in return for certain considerations. And part will be from the company's profits. But the greater part will be paid, indirectly, by that thieving Chinese, for none of the ransom that he paid me went through the company's accounts.'

Commodore Tasman and Pilot-Major Visscher sat in the great cabin of the *Heemskerck*, reading the instructions of the Batavia Council that would govern their lives for the next year at least. The *Heemskerck* was a sailing vessel of 120 tonnes, three-masted, heavily armed, and carrying a crew of sixty. Her consort was the *Zeehaen*, a flute larger than the *Heemskerck*, not so heavily armed, and with a crew of fifty. Both ships were square-rigged on main and fore with a lateen mizen.

The instructions left little to chance. The expedition was required to seek out all known and unknown lands to the south, to trace their coasts and make charts of the passages towards them.

'We're not going to have much time for brooding,' Abel said.

'Listen to this.' Visscher read the document. ' "You are to discover the unreached South and Eastern Land and any convenient passages to known rich places for the general increase of the company's welfare." '

'A fine tall order, but typical lawyers work.' Abel grunted.

'Yes, everything worded in such a way that we can discover nothing to benefit ourselves.'

'And the sailing instructions! It's a wonder they don't

tell us when to shorten sail. Talk of teaching your grand-mother to suck eggs!'

'Well, I don't mind them telling us to go to Mauritius,' said Francis. 'There are some doubtful islands in the Indian Ocean we can look for on the way. And it's easier to run before the westerlies than to beat against them.'

'And it's nice of them not to want us to go south of 54°!' said Abel.

'If we can get that far, in those waters.'

'And we are to run northwards in the longitude of the Solomon Islands.'

Both men laughed, for no two mapmakers could agree exactly what or where the Solomon Islands were.

'I see we will have two merchants on board,' Abel said. 'Isaac Gilsemans and Abraham Coomans. I don't know either of them.'

'I know Mynheer Gilsemans. No seaman, but a good trader and shipmate. If there's anything to be made, Isaac will find it.'

'Then there's only one more thing we have to do—and that is to find out whether New Guinea is one land or two.'

'Which really means finding out whether de Torres was right in reporting a strait. Heavens! You could not find out all they want to know in six voyages.'

'And we'll be victualled for only nine months. Well, we can only do as much as we can.'

'And if that's not enough,' said Visscher, 'they will have to send someone else.'

At the house by the canal Jannetie prepared Abel's clothes for the long voyage. She had knitted him thick stockings and ganseys, which was weary work in tropical Batavia, but she knew that south, where Abel was going, it would be bitter weather. She made pickles and conserves to flavour the food, trying all the while not to think how lonely she would be without him.

They rarely spoke of their many separations, and one day Abel surprised her. 'At sea,' he said, 'I never think how

long it has been since I left you. I wake each morning thinking this is one day nearer my return.'

Jannetie laughed. 'You are away just as long, however
you look at it.'

'Maybe, but isn't it better to look forward with hope
than back with regret?'

The flotilla sailed for Mauritius on 14th August 1642.
They did not have a good start, for that evening *Zeehaen*
went aground off the Isle of Rotterdam, and was not
refloated until the morning watch next day. There seemed
little damage to the hull or rigging, but a stranding had to
be logged. Her captain, Gerrit Janszoon, was new to the
ship, and could not be expected to know everything about
his command.

'Just so long as he does not make the same mistake twice,'
Abel said to Visscher, as he made the log entry. 'I wish I
could have had Gerrit Demmer for skipper.'

Three days later Abel flew the signal to call his council.
Dutchmen were great believers in councils, even to advise
commodores on voyages of discovery. It was a golden afternoon. The Prince Islands lay to southward, while the hill
of Krakatoa dwindled astern. They were clear of the shoals
and coral of the Straits of Sunda, and an expanse of ocean
lay ahead. There might be a few small islands between
them and Africa, but there could be nothing of any size.

With seven members on the Voyage Council, there was
no chance of a tied vote. Abel was president and Abraham
Coomans, under-merchant in the *Heemskerck*, was
secretary. Jude Tjercsen and Visscher, skipper and mate of
the *Heemskerck*, were members, as were Gerrit Janszoon,
Hendrik Pieterszoon and Isaac Gilsemans of the *Zeehaen*.

Francis Visscher was a year or so older than Abel, and the
best chartmaker in the Indies. But he was not as good a
seaman as his commodore, and was quite happy to serve as
mate and pilot-major. What he lacked in seamanship he
made up for in skill as a surveyor. He had sailed in Chinese
junks to survey the coast around Tonkin. He had also

surveyed the Isle of Hainan and some of the Japanese coast, until the shogun had objected. While making these trips, his ability as a seaman had suffered, and he hoped this voyage would restore it.

The other skippers and mates were all junior to Abel, and knew that their future with the company depended on his reports. 'Tasman's luck' was becoming proverbial in the Indies, and men were still chuckling at the abduction of Eng Po Tang. Abel was sure of the loyalty of his deck officers.

He was not so sure of the merchants, Gilsemans and Coomans. They served in a different branch of the company. Some of this branch had all the arrogance of those whose work does not soil the hands. Abel could have done without them, even though Coomans made a good secretary. That trade followed the flag and did not accompany it was as true in 1642 as it had been in the days of Columbus. Abel guessed they were on board to make a report to the Merchants Federation, and it might be a biased one. It was said a man had nothing to fear from the truth, but he resolved to be meticulous in keeping his private journal.

Abel thought of having a word with Visscher about the merchants, but decided not to. His pilot was from Flushing, and had been in the Indies longer than himself. If a Flushing man could not look after himself, then nobody could.

The council gathered in the great cabin of the *Heemskerck*, Janszoon and Pieterszoon keeping anxious watch on their ship following astern. There were the familiar sounds : the creaking of tiller and whipstaff, and the gurgle of water round the rudder. It was one of those exhilarating days at sea, with a fresh breeze blowing and the deck-head reflecting patterns of light from the sun playing on the blue water.

'Just to begin,' Abel said, blowing smoke from his pipe, 'I'd like to hear from Captain Janszoon a report of any damage his ship suffered from her stranding.'

'It was not my fault. That damned coral—'

'No one is blaming you, captain ! The Dutch skipper who

has never scraped the putty has yet to be born. But was there any damage?'

Slightly mollified, Gerrit Janszoon said, 'She may have carried away a bit of cladding, but there's no leak. The shock sprung the fore-topmast, but that's been repaired by the carpenters.'

'H'm! Well, we'll have time in Mauritius to put her on the beach and fix the cladding.' The cladding consisted of thin planks nailed over the bottom, with a coating of tar and sheep's wool between them and the true planking. 'I wouldn't want to sail with the cladding damaged in either ship. That would make it an open go for the teredo worm, if anything would. You can indent for some labour ashore, so there need be no extra work for anyone but the carpenter and his mates.'

'Do the idlers good,' said Pieterszoon. Idlers were the craftsmen in a ship, who did not normally keep a watch.

'The carpenters from both ships could work together,' said Jude Tjercsen. 'Didn't you say we were only to be in Mauritius for a fortnight?'

'That's the present plan. After all, the sooner we get to where we're going, the sooner we get back to Batavia.'

'Even though we don't know where it is, eh!' said Tjercsen. There was a rumble of laughter before Abel spoke again.

'I've only sailed this way once before, five years ago in the old *Banda*, and no doubt some of you know these ports a good deal better than I do. Now this is my sailing plan. We were in 6°20′ south at noon. I propose to sail south-west by west as far as 14° south, then turn west-south-west to 20° south. This should give us steady easterly trades on the beam; then we can run our westing down until we sight Mauritius.'

There were only minor objections to this, some contending that the south-west by west course should be held farther to the south in the interests of faster sailing.

Visscher, as pilot-major, answered this. 'If this were an

ordinary trading voyage, I would agree. But we are on a voyage of discovery. One reason for the dog-leg course is to look for the Keeling Islands, sighted by a captain of the English company thirty years ago.'

'I've heard of them,' said Captain Janszoon, 'but they cannot be very big.'

'They could still be rich in pearls,' said Isaac Gilsemans.

'And if we find them we can stay a day or so to fix the longitude,' said Visscher. 'They will make a good departure point for future voyages. And there's a rumour of another island two hundred leagues east of Mauritius; that's the reason for our long westerly run.'

There was some discussion, but no dissension. 'See that the course is entered in the journals of both ships,' said Abel, 'and the following general order, on which there will be no discussion. Since I hope to sail beyond all charting, it is important we remain in company and that at least some of us arrive back in Batavia. A discovery not reported might as well never have been made. So, at sunset the ships will close to within four cables of one another, then shorten sail down to the courses. Each ship will carry a lighted lantern at the mainmast, as well as the customary one astern. The watch on deck will be allowed to sleep on their posts, except the helmsman and the lookouts who should not do more than one hour's duty each.'

'Hear, hear! I'm all for making less work during the silent hours.' Gerrit Janszoon agreed with Abel's plan.

'Yes, there's nothing to be gained by tiring the men. Later on we might experiment with having them in three watches, so that every third night each watch will get a full night's sleep.'

So all was ordered for the passage to Mauritius, and the visitors returned to their ship.

2

New Land

FOR nineteen days they saw nothing other than flying-fish and sea phosphorescence at night. Sometimes the ships were close enough to exchange hails, sometimes so far apart that all one could see of the other was the lift and flash of a distant topsail.

No islands were sighted, and except for the aftermath of a distant storm at the end of August they had smooth sailing. It was a sailors holiday, for even the storm was pleasant. It brought torrents of soft rain, which meant that there was much bathing and washing of clothes, leaving the sea stained with soapsuds for half an acre round each ship.

There were five ships at Fort Frederik Hendrik when they had threaded their way through the coral that fringed the entry to the port of Mauritius. This meant that there would be news from home and old shipmates to be met on shore.

'I don't know why the company bothers with this place,' Francis said to Abel, as they proceeded ashore to pay their duty call on van der Stel, the governor. 'The summer climate is foul, and what isn't solid rock is either jungle or swamp.'

'It has good water, Francis, and jungle can be cleared, while solid rock is better than swamp.'

'The water is as good at the Cape of Good Hope, which has a better anchorage, no coral reefs, and suitable land for market gardens. The Cape is also easier to find from the sea.'

'We found this easily enough.'

'Yes, we did. But wait till we want to leave!'

'What do you mean?'

'We came in with a fair wind, but it was a trade wind blowing the same way eight days out of ten. It could still be blowing when we want to leave, and we might be a week getting to sea. That's why I say we should leave Mauritius to the rats and move to the Cape.'

For the repairs to the *Zeehaen*, Governor van der Stel gave what aid he could, which was little enough. With five ships in the anchorage and a French pirate reported to be stealing ebonywood from the other side of the island, he had plenty on his hands. Tasman's ships were not the only ones at the fort with damage to be fixed, but van der Stel lent him six men. Even so, most of the work would have to be done by the crew.

'A change is as good as a rest,' Abel said, as he and the captains juggled with the watch bills. 'Let's try it this way, a quarter of the crew will help the carpenters and provide an anchor watch; two men from each ship will be cooper's mates, because I want extra water-casks made; the rest can go ashore with the under-mates, cutting wood in the jungle, roasting charcoal and distilling tar from the trimmings. We will have a changeover twice a week, except for the cooper's mates.'

'The carpenters won't like that—training a new gang twice a week.'

'I've been twenty years at sea, and chippies are always the same—full of complaints. But these orders stand. We don't know what is in front of us, except that it will probably be unpleasant. I want all hands to be rested as much as possible, and, after all, the chippies don't keep a watch at sea.'

Abel knew that a timber-cutting party was looked on as a holiday by the average seaman, because of the unlimited fresh water and the fresh food that usually went with it, whereas labouring on a ship's bottom in water to the waist was hard, hot and dirty work. Not that timber-getting parties would find much fresh meat. Game on the island was both scarce and shy. But delicious fruits grew wild for the picking. These activities kept them at Mauritius for a month; then they were weatherbound for three days, awaiting a wind to take them offshore. The wind was so strong that they could not even kedge themselves out with anchor and cable—and it has to be a strong wind to prevent a sixty-man crew from kedging out a hundred-tonne ship.

Once out of the harbour they had flying-fish weather as far as 30° south, when the trades failed them and the weather turned cooler. But they made progress every day but one, when they struck a flat calm and drifted back the way they had come for about three leagues. Sometimes there was too much wind, so that they had to reef down or heave to under a storm-sail to avoid being swamped by the huge swells. It was difficult to keep a footing, in spite of lifelines being rigged on the spar-deck. This was a time when the men were glad of the ganseys and stockings knitted by their womenfolk in Batavia. There were some Javanese in the crew, and they became almost useless, shivering with cold in their thin cotton clothing.

One consolation was that so much rain and hail meant fresh water was never a problem. During these days there was no light-hearted skylarking as the casks were filled. It was too cold for bathing, and if clothes had been washed they could not be dried. To hang them in the open was to have them whipped to shreds or torn from the line, and the living quarters became dank caves hung with garments that never seemed to dry.

Only once did the ships lose sight of each other, and there was great rejoicing when they came upon one another a day later. On the passage to Mauritius the ships had a ready-made rendezvous had they become separated, but now that was impossible. They were in unknown seas with only guessed-at land before them, and it was vital that they stayed in touch.

Abel thanked God daily that they did so, for like many

sailors he felt that he was at all times in the hands of God. He prayed each day, while some of the Javanese lit incense or butter-lamps at their own little shrines. Abel did not forbid this; he had seen enough intolerance of religion in Europe not to want it to follow his ships into the Southern Ocean.

There were times when he felt they had reached the end of the world. But there was always another waste of grey-green water ahead. They reached 45° south; as far south of the equator as Bordeaux, in France, was north of it. One day they sailed seventy leagues, and almost as far on a number of others. But such sailing meant damage to rigging and spars, extra shrouds to be rigged, sheets and lifts to be spliced and rerove, and cheek pieces fitted to sprung spars.

It was about these strains that Abel spoke one day to his pilot-major.

'Our orders from the council,' he said, 'require us to press on to 50° south before heading east. I doubt if either ship will stand it.'

'Schouten and le Maire went to 55° south when they discovered Cape Horn thirty years ago.'

'It must have been better weather than this! I'm at the point of believing the old philosophers: that the earth is flat and if we go much farther we shall sail over the edge!'

'Well, there's not much sign of the Great South Land,' said Francis alluding to the belief held at the time that a great landmass must lie south of the equator to balance the weight of the land north of it. 'Looking at the rollers, I feel there's no land for hundreds of leagues in any direction. These swells are too even to have ever known a shore.'

'There could be land to the east, but we'd never know about it until struck,' Abel replied.

'Then when we start to run our easting down, we must keep double lookouts.'

'Don't worry! We're doing that now.' Abel flew the flag to summon his council, streaming a cable astern so that *Zeehaen* could secure to it while her officers came to the *Heemskerck*. But the seas ran so high that to launch a boat would have been madness. So a council-in-little was held in the flagship, and the decisions passed across the water by a speaking-trumpet.

They altered course next day to the south-east, being 45°43′ south latitude, and the ships sailed easier at once, with the wind on the quarter. Abel determined to go as far south as possible on this course, for as long as the ships could endure the buffeting.

They had left the flying-fish far to the north, and were now followed day and night by albatrosses, riding the air-waves astern with scarcely a flicker of their wingtips. Despite their noble appearance, they swept down screaming over the tubs of galley scraps emptied over the rail by the cooks, so that the crew swore they were the ghosts of hungry seamen. For this same reason no one shot at them, although the pounds of fresh meat each carried would have been very welcome.

Their first death of the voyage was when the master-gunner died suddenly in his sleep. Abel recorded it in the journal, and sadly read the service over him as they slid the canvas-shrouded body over the side. He knew that this death might be the first of many.

'I've said before,' said Francis Visscher, 'that if land lies to the south, it must be hundreds of leagues away—and so frozen and barren as to be useless either for trade or for settlement.'

'There could be fur or whale-oil,' replied Abraham Coomans. 'God knows it is cold enough in Muscovy or Iceland, but Muscovy is rich in furs and there have been fortunes made at the whale fishery.'

'There are certain differences in the situation,' said Abel. 'There are Dutch ports within easy sail of both Muscovy and Iceland in the summer, and a summer voyage round the North Cape is no great hardship. We are approaching summer in these latitudes now.'

'At a time of year equal to the Dutch spring,' said Francis. 'Can you see a tulip as much as sprout in weather like this, even if there were ground for it to sprout in?'

It was early afternoon, and the wooden deadlights were closed over the stern-windows, shuddering every so often to the impact of the sea. Only a greyness came through the skylights, and lamps had been lit so that the charts could be read. Standing lit in a tray of gravel, a charcoal stove did little to dispel the camp chill. Those present wore woollen mittens and their faces were chapped with cold.

'There's little pleasure in these parts,' said Abel, 'though it is said that the man who goes to sea for pleasure would go to hell for pastime.' He laughed and took a pull at the mug of hot schnapps and lemon he held. 'But to get back to business. I think we have pressed as far south as is safe.'

'Or farther, if you ask me,' said Jude Tjercsen, 'and I'll warrant that our friends in the *Zeehaen* think the same. Not a day passes but we're repairing chafed rigging or sprung spars.'

'I know. So I propose to sail north-east to about 40°, then east again to the longitude of the Solomon Islands.'

'Ah!' said one of the under-mates, 'but do we know where they are?'

'Well, they've been reported in three different places,' said Francis. 'They are certainly somewhere, and we shall find them. Once found, we'll fix their longitude by lunar sights, and pin them down for all time.'

'Hear, hear!'

'I've called this council because I want an agreement to go against the orders of the Batavia Council.' Abel's face was stern. 'They are explicit that we proceed to 54° south. That's not feasible, as anyone can see who cares to step on deck.'

'Orders like that should never be given,' said Jude Tjercsen.

'I wish the people from the *Zeehaen* could be here, to help us decide,' said Abraham Coomans.

'They'd agree with us,' said Abel. 'They're in the same situation as ourselves: strained rigging, sprung spars, and broken bones.'

'We could hold to the south another week—'

'A week to the south means another week getting back to where we are now! We could hold on until we had solved all the secrets of the five oceans and the seven seas! We could lose the ships and die in the doing. Then who would be the wiser, if we never returned to say what we had seen?'

Abel became silent, looking hard at each man around the table. 'Does anyone really think we should press on to the south? Come on, this is the time to speak. Francis? Jude? Mynheer Coomans? Everyone else?'

No one spoke. 'Well, silence gives consent, and we'd get the same answer from the *Zeehaen*. Now write this down, Mynheer Coomans, and make a copy to float across to *Zeehaen* on the end of a line. I want there to be no mis-understandings.'

With oiled silk and beeswax the acting-gunner water-proofed a shot-case with the orders inside, and it took two hours to float it across to the other ship. It took, however, less than ten minutes for the message to be read and the stadtholder's flag dipped in acknowledgement. *Heemskerck* fired a gun, and bore away nor'easterly on the new course. To the weary crews it seemed as if the ship already moved easier.

The turbulent weather lasted until 24th November, when the wind and sea both eased. The decks dried out in the sun, and clothes could be dried at last. Reefs were shaken out of the topsails, and a bonnet laced to the foot of the main-courses. Springtime had come again. Two days later *Heemskerck* paid for her racking drive through the roaring forties as the rudder-stock snapped where it entered the hull. The carpenters worked like heroes that day, up to their waists in icy water. Somehow they shaped and bolted a fishplate on either side of the break, and by late afternoon the ship was under way again.

Almost immediately afterwards the lookouts in both ships sighted land. New land, that no European eye had ever seen before. Soon it was visible from the deck, and the showers of sleet could not keep the men below. They could see a wild coast, with high cliffs and towering mountains rising behind. An old memory nagged at Abel as he gazed. Then he remembered the hills—no, mountains—he had seen when he walked the Fife shore in Scotland years ago with Gerrit Demmer. He wished Gerrit could have been with him now, to look upon these mountains at the other side of the world. He gave Jude and Francis a delighted grin.

'New land, lads, new land! What are we going to call it?'

3

Van Diemen's Land

'THERE can be only one name for it,' said Visscher. 'And that's Tasman's Land.'

'No, no. If it must be named after a person, it should be Governor van Diemen. After all, without his influence none of us would be here,' Abel said.

As if to welcome them to the new land the weather turned mild, with a gentle three-knot breeze. One league offshore they took a sounding, finding sixty fathoms of water with a bottom of broken coral and shell. Closer inshore the depth was the same, too great to come to anchor off an unknown coast.

They hove-to well out of danger from the land that night, but within sight of it. Next morning Abel summoned a council as they cruised slowly to the south-east. It was a happy meeting, now that they were clear of the foul weather, and a new land lay smiling under the lee. Today in the great cabin the deadlights were hooked back, and the air was filled with a tang carried out by an eddy from the shore. There was something in it of fresh turpentine, but less pungent and more spicy. It was a pleasant change from the reek of wet garments and stale bilges that had filled their noses for the past two months. Contentedly the men sat round the table, puffing clouds of smoke from long clay pipes.

'There is no doubt that this land is new,' Abel said, 'but we do not know whether it is part of New Holland or not. I have decided that we name it for the governor.'

There was a chorus of approval, and Gerrit Janszoon

said, 'Now we've begun, no doubt we shall be finding other lands. Let's hope there will be enough to name one after each of us!'

'So long as the largest is named for the governor,' said Isaac Gilsemans.

'The first, but we do not know whether it is the largest, for there is no way of knowing, with the time at our disposal, whether what we see are islands or capes. So I move that each new feature we find from now is named by lot, drawn from a hat by the youngest on board.'

After this decision they celebrated their discovery by drinking the stadtholder's and Governor van Diemen's health with a great bowl of punch, made from the last of the limes they had brought all the way from Mauritius. When the toasts and celebration were over, Abel brought the meeting to order and they proceeded with business. Naturally he was in favour of making a landing as soon as possible.

'We've sailed so long by guess and by God that we might be hundreds of leagues out in our longitude. We need to fix our position by lunar sights to get a new point of departure—as well as filling the water-casks and seeing what the land has to offer in the way of replenishments.'

'And find out what sort of people live there, and the chances of trade,' said Isaac Gilsemans.

'The safety of the ships comes first,' Abel spoke firmly. 'And we must know where we are, so that others may follow us.'

Turning towards the land, they found good anchorage at the mouth of a sound, twenty-two fathoms deep, with a bottom of fine sand. After sunset they gathered in the *Heemskerck* to give thanks to God for preserving their lives and bringing them to this new land.

At dawn next morning Abel watched the two longboats with sixteen well-armed men under the command of Francis Visscher pull away from the shore. He would have liked to lead the party himself, but held back knowing his first duty was the safety of the ships. There was plenty of work to do on board, but Abel ordered a make-and-mend for the afternoon, and the crew spent this free time either sleeping or fishing. Abel could no neither: if he fished alongside the men it would spoil their sport, and his mind was too active for him to sleep. He would have played chess, but Visscher was his usual opponent and none of the other officers on board knew the game. In the end he played himself, right hand against left, but it was a pointless exercise.

It was late in the afternoon before the boats returned. Abel heard the boats hook onto the chains, and a babble of talk at the entry port. He put the chessmen away and, taking his hat, left the cabin to go on deck.

That evening the ship was filled with the pleasant smell of broiling fish. More sat down to eat in the *Heemskerck*'s cabin than usual, for some of the *Zeehaen* people had come over to hear Francis Visscher speak of his adventures ashore. It was a good supper, with mussel sauce to go with the fish and pot herbs and greens. Some of the greens were like those that grew at the Cape of Good Hope, others were not familiar. The cook had boiled these with salt and a silver spoon in the pot, and since the spoon did not blacken had concluded they were fit to eat. They drank arrack and molasses with this meal, for the wine had soured and the shore expedition had found no lemons. After the meal they sat back to listen to Visscher.

'There's nothing much to report, shipmates,' came his voice from behind a puff of smoke. 'You've eaten the mussels and the greens, and there wasn't much else.'

'There must be wood and water,' said Abel, thinking of the needs of the ship.

'There were many small creeks, but we found no sizeable stream. It will take a long time to fill the casks. As to the trees, Peter Jacobs the carpenter was with me, and we felled some to bring the timber on board. They are hard and resinous, and the bark scales off easily. Also, they weep a kind of gum.' He rummaged in a pocket. 'Here, I brought some with me.'

'May I see it?' asked Isaac Gilsemans. 'Gums and lacquers are a good start for trade.'

'We'll take samples back and let the experts have a look at them,' said Abel. 'And we'll roast some of the wood for charcoal, and see what sort of tar and turpentine we get from it. The turpentine should be good. I've been smelling it in the air ever since we found the coast. Did you see any sign of men?'

'Signs, but that was all. There were notches cut in some of the trees, though whether they were cut in order to reach the tops for fruits, we could not decide.'

'You did not go up to find out?'

'It would have been difficult. The people who cut the steps must be very different from us, or very much taller. The notches were about five feet apart.' There was a murmur of astonishment. 'Yet we were in no doubt that they were cut as steps, with some sort of chisel or adze. Oh, and we saw smoke.'

'We saw smoke from here,' said Jude Tjercsen, 'but it might have been your own fire.'

'We only lit one, to cook some mussel broth at midday. How much smoke did you see?'

'I counted six fires, but some said there were more.'

'They'd be signal fires, no doubt,' said Abraham Coomans. 'I've heard that the Indians at New Amsterdam settlement speak together with smoke signals.'

'We can take it, then, there are men ashore,' said Abel. 'Did you see any beasts or game?'

'We saw tracks like tiger marks, only smaller, and pelleted dung larger than that of a rabbit.'

'Well, that's hopeful. If there are tigers there must be something for them to eat, and what a tiger can eat, so can we!'

'That thought struck me too, so we looked for a drinking-place, without success. Though we did not go far from the beach.'

'From the ship the forest seems to grow right down to

the sands,' said Gerrit Janszoon.

'It does, and I think the trees are evergreen, for the odd leaf was fluttering down all the time, but there was no drift of leaf mould round the trunks, nor grass in the glades between them. All the trees are sparsely leaved, and give little shade. We also heard music.'

'Music!'

'Yes, like a peal of bells or a set of gongs.'

'Maybe a birdcall? There's a night bird in Java with a call like a gong stroke.'

'It could be,' said Francis. 'I was so eager to find men I forgot that birds have voices too!'

'You've done well,' said Abel. 'We'll fill the water-casks tomorrow and try to find out more about the people. Surely they must be there.'

They filled some of the casks next day, but with difficulty. There were no deep pools in the stream-beds, and the rock they ran through was so hard that it would have taken a blast of gunpowder to dig a settling-pit.

'Never mind,' Abel said, 'there will, no doubt, be better watering-places farther on. We have enough water to go on with, and plenty of charcoal and firewood. But before doing anything else, we must take formal possession of this coast.'

'We should have done that the first day.'

'Well, we'll do it now. I've had a stake prepared, and we'll set it firmly ashore, above the tidemark.'

'In the name of the company?'

'In the name of the United Provinces, *and* the company, engraved on a lead plate, with the stadtholder's flag flying over it.'

'When you say we, do you mean me to do this?' Francis queried.

'You've led all the shore parties up to now.'

'But not this one, Abel. You are the commodore.'

Abel looked at his commodore's pennant fluttering at the peak of the mizen. This was true. He had been too concerned with the safety of the ships, and it was his duty to take possession of the new land. The title to the land, in fact, might not be legal unless he did so.

'Yes,' he said, 'sometimes I become too concerned over the ships. We'll do the job tomorrow. I will nail up the tablet, and you shall raise the flag!'

Next day the offshore breeze combined with a strong surf and made it impossible to land from a boat.

'We shall have to wait for calmer weather,' Abel announced.

The carpenter Peter Jacobs had been giving the situation some thought.

'The sea is warm and I swim well,' he said. 'Take in the boat as far as possible, and lie on the oars. I'll swim ashore with the stake and flag.'

'You can't carry them and swim as well.'

Peter produced a coil of cord. 'The stake is wood, so it will float and carry the tools and the flag. I'll tie one end of this round my waist, and the other to the stake.' He stripped off his outer clothing and dropped over the side in his shirt and drawers, then swam ashore, shooting through the surf with the stake a safe distance behind him. He set the stake and flag firmly in the ground in front of a grove of trees on a small knoll, tied the tools across his shoulders and, plunging into the surf, swam back to the boat.

While Peter dressed and swallowed a dram of arrack, Abel spoke. 'That must be the first time a discoverer has taken possession of a land without ever setting foot on it. We will give our thanks to God in the old way of the sea, watch-and-watch. We will say the twenty-fourth psalm, starboard taking the first verse. This is the psalm the Romans call *Domini est Terra*, and it begins, "The earth is the Lord's and the fullness thereof, the world and those who dwell therein." ' Abel read out each verse, starboard or larboard thwartsmen chanting them after him. And so the words of thanksgiving rolled out, to be lost in the sound of the wind and the sea, while from a distance the dark eyes of the inhabitants looked down with wonder at the actions of these strangers.

The weather became more blustery on the following day, and started the anchors dragging. They had named the place where the stake was set up, Frederik Hendrik Bay, in honour of the stadtholder, but now it was time to leave it. When one of the anchors was raised, the iron flukes were found to have been pulled almost straight with the stock. There was little peace that day as the smith and his mates set up the forge in the well-deck, repairing the damage with new iron fashioned by mighty blows of the sledge-hammer.

The coast trended more and more to the north, and the wind blew ever more strongly from the west. There was no chance of reaching the land, which was maddening, since the smoke of signal fires could be seen as far as the eye could see. Abel had to make a difficult decision. Five days was a ridiculously short time to spend on a new coast, especially when it seemed certain that men lived there. On the other hand, there were his orders from the council to sail to the Solomons, either to find the east coast of New Holland from there, or discover the extent of the islands, or else find an easterly route to the coast of Chile. Whatever he did, the odds were against him. But the Solomons venture, Francis and he agreed, had the best chance of succeeding.

They were victualled for only eight months, and if they spent too long on this new coast they might have trouble getting back to Batavia. Abel had set Van Diemen's Land firmly on the charts, so that a later expedition could come in his track and spend more time there. He was disappointed, though, not to find out more about this land. He had the signal flown to call a council.

Four hours later the weather had worsened to such an extent that they were blown off the coast. Abel remembered the Portuguese ships being blown off the Japanese coast and finding the Gold and Silver Islands, and hoped this was a good omen for himself. Anything might exist in these foreign seas.

'That confirms our decision,' said Francis at his side. The council had suggested holding northward until nightfall, before turning from the coast. 'It's eastward ho, whether we like it or not. Well, I've always had a curiosity about the Solomons.'

'Me too,' said Jude Tjercsen, who was not married. 'I wonder what the girls are like there?'

'Girls!' Abel feigned impatience with the younger man. 'I don't care if they've all got faces like a burst sea boot— so long as there are some good springs of fresh water.'

4

Murderers' Bay

THEY saw the last of Van Diemen's Land on 5th December 1642. For three days after they sailed with fair winds from the west, under blue skies and over tumbling seas. It was pleasant sailing weather, fresh enough to give a man an appetite. Apart from the shortage of water—no deep-sea commodore likes the drumming of empty casks in the orlop —Abel was satisfied with the voyage so far. The slow passage along the coast had allowed the crews to make good all the damage sustained in the roaring forties, and he cast about in his mind for something to add interest to the day's work. Then he saw two sacks of gravel, left over from a load that had been brought aboard to replace the grease-spattered stuff in the tray under the galley-stove. Two men were about to sway it below to join the other gravel in the ballast when Abel stopped them, at the same time summoning Jan Lydekker, the newly promoted master-gunner.

'How long is it since the men were exercised at the guns, Jan?'

'Never at the swivels, commodore. And for the great guns, not since the day after we left Fort Frederik Hendrik.'

'I was not thinking of the great guns,' replied Abel. 'We are unlikely to run into pirates in these waters. I was thinking of the *steenstuks*—the swivels. Some of the Solomons are hostile, and a few rounds from the swivels might save us from being boarded and butchered.'

'True enough,' said the master-gunner, his eyes lighting with professional keenness. 'Though if we were attacked, it might be better to let the savages board amidships, then clear the deck with fire from the poop and forecastle. All right, mynheer commodore, gun-drill with the swivels it shall be!'

'For shot you may use the gravel in sacks under the gratings, if you think it suitable.'

'Yes, in fact, my mates have already stitched some of it up in bags to use as case-shot.'

'You don't think it will damage the guns?'

'Mynheer, *nothing* could damage those guns. It might even improve them by scouring out the barrels!'

The swivel guns were captured Spanish pieces, with barrels forged from iron bars strengthened with shrunk-on rings of the same metal. They were breech-loaders after the old pattern, with bronze breeches secured by knock-out wedges in a trough behind the barrel. With a handful of powder they threw a two-pound bag of shot or gravel far enough to deter would-be boarders. Many a crew in wild seas owed their lives to the swivels, the crews of which required little training.

There is nothing a seaman enjoys more than target practice. Each ship launched towed targets made from old casks ballasted to float upright, each carrying a black-and-yellow flag and veered astern at a quarter-cable length. The Spanish colours were black and yellow, and Dutchmen were always happy to fire on them, even if only in play. Little damage could be done to the casks at that range, for swivels were not intended to batter in ships' sides. Splinters could fly, however, and at times a lucky shot would rend the flag to tatters. Willing hands then hauled in the target to replace the marker, and the forenoon's work was good for the men. Bets were won and lost, and many a plug of tobacco changed hands that morning. The crews dismissed to the midday meal in high humour.

The wind freshened the next day and summer was banished by storms of rain and sleet. Sails with a hose stitched into the centre were spread to trap the downpour, and when the salt had been washed from the canvas the precious water was run into casks. After that there was a great washing of clothes, though only the hardiest bathed.

The storm abated and they had another three days of good sailing weather. Then, on 13th December, the look-outs saw mountains on the skyline, the second new land in three weeks.

'There are three possibilities,' Abel said, when the ships had been hove-to and the council met together. 'The first is that this land we see is a large island, for it would seem unlikely that a small one would have such high mountains. The second is that it is a peninsula stemming from the Great South Land of the philosophers—'

'Why that?' asked Isaac Gilsemans. 'Why a peninsula?'

'Three weeks ago we were almost in 50° south, and the pilot and I were sure there was no land within hundreds of leagues to the south. In a way this conclusion is strengthened by the voyage of Schouten and le Maire thirty years back, who rounded Cape Horn and could see no land to the south either. If this in front of us is part of the Great South Land it must be a sudden upthrust, for we are now in 45° south. Does that reasoning seem good to you, mynheer?'

'Yes,' said the merchant. 'It's good enough until we know better.'

'Thank you, Isaac,' said Abel, and returned to his argument. 'The third possibility is that it is part of Van Diemen's Land.'

'Surely not!' said Gerrit Janszoon. 'What about the open water we have sailed since we left there?'

'Suppose you sailed south from Ushant and your next landfall was Finisterre. These are not two separate lands, but both are part of Europe, with the Bay of Biscay in between. It may be the same here.'

The skipper nodded, for this made sense.

'There's one way of finding out the truth,' said Francis Visscher, 'and that's by sailing south. If it's a peninsula, then by going south we shall find the mainland—the South Land—'

'If it exists!' said Abel.

'If this is an island,' Francis Visscher continued, 'we could sail round it by following the coast until we come back to where we started from. If it is part of Van Diemen's Land, we should round its southern tip, and join up with the mainland somewhere to the north.'

'And which of these would you do?' asked Jude Tjercsen, when he had puzzled out Francis's statement.

'I'd like to sail south,' replied Francis, 'hoping that what lies before us is an island. I've no real belief in a Great South Land, at least not one of any use to mankind. If there is land down there, it must be as barren as Novaya Zembla or Greenland in the Arctic.'

'You are getting away from the point, Francis,' Abel interjected. 'We were not sent here to find the South Land, but to find the east coast of New Holland. I propose, therefore, that we explore this coast to the north, leaving its southerly extent to be determined by a later voyage.'

'I incline to the pilot's view,' said Abraham Coomans. 'You will recall I was for pressing to the south once before.'

'And if we had,' said Francis, 'we might never have found Van Diemen's Land.'

'And northward, say I,' said Gerrit Janszoon. 'As the commodore says, our orders are to find the east coast of New Holland.'

There was little more to be said, for there is a great tendency to obey orders when they coincide with inclination. Only the under-merchant, Abraham Coomans, raised a voice in favour of going south, giving no particular reason for his view. Abel looked at him narrowly, wondering what was in his mind.

For five days they probed the new coast, anchoring at night if they could, and proceeding slowly under reefed topsails where there was no anchorage. All felt that the land was inhabited, since from the second night they had seen the gleam of fires ashore. It was 18th December before they saw any other sign of life. They anchored about a league from land that evening, and Visscher and Isaac Gilsemans set off to shore in order to find fresh water. Though the casks had been filled during the squall a few days earlier, the contents had blackened and soured. Only the little water they had left from Van Diemen's Land was still sweet. The ships lay in a wide bay, with land on three sides of it, and the declining sun was almost hidden by cliffs to the west. There was the glow of fires ashore, and through his telescope Abel could see four boats drawn up on the beach. He was pleased about this. Men who could build boats had skills, and skills meant they might have goods for trade. The possession of boats, in fact, implied some sort of trade.

It was getting quite dark when they saw the flash of oars as Visscher's boats pulled out from the beach. Francis was first at the entry-port, and Abel greeted him. 'Well, master-pilot, what did you find?'

'An interesting-looking land, commodore, but the people stood on shore with weapons at hand to oppose a landing.'

A dozen seamen stood near, ears pricked to catch what they could. Isaac Gilsemans climbed aboard, and Abel said, seriously, 'You had better come where we can talk.'

In the great cabin he poured a drink for all of them. 'Now, what were these people like?' he continued.

'Stoutly built, as we are, and about the same height. Reddish-brown—'

'And seamen, or boatmen, anyway. It was their boats drawn up on the beach?'

'Yes, big double-hulled canoes, fifteen or twenty metres long and very well built. Some had a mast and sail, and a kind of matting hut on the thwarts connecting the hulls. And the men—reddish-brown skins, with black hair coiled in a topknot.'

Abel had heard of Indians of the New Amsterdam settlements who were said to be warlike and who built good canoes. He called for his Javanese servant. 'Kattai, pass the word quickly for a council, and summon the master-gunner to attend. Quickly, we may not have much time!'

Half an hour later two canoes lay a short distance from the ships, the men in them calling out in deep voices. They stayed just out of range of the swivel guns and seemed to know it, for they would come no nearer. None of the Dutch could understand what they said.

Even Isaac Gilsemans was baffled. 'I can speak eight different Eastern tongues,' he said, 'as well as Dutch, Spanish, German, English and French. But this is Greek to me!' And he laughed at his own joke.

'Listen! Is that a trumpet-call?' said Abel.

'A conch shell,' said Francis. 'They were blowing them on the beach.'

'One of the under-mates has a bugle. Have him reply to their horn-playing, following the notes as closely as he can.'

For an hour the two sounds, like question and answer, echoed between ship and canoe. Then the notes from the conch shells grew fainter as the canoes drifted off, until there was silence when they reached the firelit shore.

There was no moon until almost dawn, or Abel would have upanchored and left there and then. But to attempt to leave an almost landlocked bay in total darkness was too great a risk.

Jan Lydekker, master-gunner, cleared and reloaded each swivel in turn. Lookouts were posted all round the ship. Musketoons and pikes were issued from the arms-chest, and word was passed that the watch on deck could sleep on their arms. Not many did.

Soon after dawn Abel saw, through the telescope, a canoe approaching. It had no sail, and the double hulls were very deep and narrow. The canoe approached the ship, but would not come nearer than half a cable's length. Cloth and knives were held up as gifts for the paddlers, but they took no notice as, chanting, they circled the ships.

'They seem to have cloth,' said Abraham Coomans. 'See

that cloak worn by the steersman? Good quality, too, by the way it hangs.'

'Still, you'd think they'd be attracted by the knives,' said Abel. 'The Formosans weave excellent cloth, but they'll always trade for cutlery.' He turned at a hail from the *Zeehaen*, the leather trumpet to his ear. 'They'd like you to go across, Mynheer Lydekker. That's the penalty of being one master-gunner between two ships.' He looked at the canoe, still circling and the paddlers still shouting. 'Maybe you should wait awhile, until we see what our visitors intend to do. And look, there are some more canoes coming out.'

'It must be some trouble with the guns, commodore. If I leave now I can be over there before the other canoes get near.'

'True enough, you had better go. *Zeehaen*'s boat is at the boom, and you can take that. Don't come back until you are sure it's safe.'

'No, commodore! I intend to be the oldest gunner in the Indies—not the boldest!'

As soon as the boat left, Abel began to doubt the wisdom of his decision. The first canoe was being joined by seven others, and they suddenly seemed very much closer. They were making for the space between the ships which were anchored a cable's length apart. There was a space of about fifty paces, in the middle, that was out of range of the swivels from either ship.

Abel later swore that these people knew the effects of swivel guns and their effective range, for when Jan Lydekker's boat reached this blind spot, the canoes turned as one and made for it. The paddlers ceased chanting and two hundred paddle blades bit white, so that the canoes seemed to fly over the water.

'Man the guns!' roared Jude Tjercsen. 'Gunners' mates, clear the larboard cannon for action!'

The swivels barked and their shot tore up the water, but not a canoe was hit. It took time to clear the greater guns for action, for these had to be loaded and run out; gunpowder absorbs moisture, and a gun left loaded over-night becomes difficult or impossible to fire. Those not taking part in the gunnery could only watch as the tragedy was acted out a hundred paces from them.

Three canoes, manned by yelling warriors, ran down Jan Lydekker's boat. There was a savage snarling noise, like a pack of wolves pulling down a wounded beast. A single shot rang out, then clubs and paddle blades rose and fell, eventually dripping with blood. The canoes drew away, leaving the boat drifting and three men struggling in the water. Jude Tjercsen, arming the longboat with a swivel, called for a crew and pulled towards the swimming men. They were Jan Lydekker and two Javanese seamen.

Now cannon-fire was opened on the retreating canoes. Again it seemed as if the natives knew the effect of cannon-shot, for they travelled shoreward well spread out and changing course at each report. Not one of the canoes was hit.

Jude Tjercsen rescued five men, three from the water and two from the boat. One of the men in the water had drowned and one in the boat was dead. Another was so injured he died before reaching the ship. Nor was there any hope of rescuing the shipmate who had been captured by the attackers, for the gunner had seen his head struck off with a stone axe when the body was dragged into a canoe.

On board, while the dead were being shrouded in canvas, the anchors were raised, and with a solemn crew the ships tacked in succession away from Murderers' Bay.

5

Water! Water!

ON the 19th December 1642 there was a second burial at
sea. Flag-shrouded and stitched into canvas, the bodies of
the murdered men lay on planks, their messmates standing
by to slide them into the sea. Weights were sewn into the
canvas to make sure the bodies would sink swiftly.

'*We therefore commit their bodies to the deep ...*' Abel
read in a flat voice from the Bible, as Francis Visscher gave
a sign for the flags to be taken from the bodies. Abel read
the final prayer, then closed the book and tucked it under
his arm. The funeral was over, the bos'n's calls shrilled,
and the men returned to their duties.

All members of the council were there for the funeral.
'Thank you for coming, mynheeren,' said Abel. 'And now
I think we should take counsel.'

Pipes were lit and punch was served in the cabin, though
the punch was only arrack and water, sweetened with
molasses. Something had to be added to the water now to
take the taste away, since it was so foul it could scarcely be
stomached by itself. Maybe the laughter was a little too
hearty, but no one mentioned the funeral they had just left.

'It has always been my way,' Abel said when his pipe
was drawing well, 'to treat the people in a new land as
friends until they proved to be enemies. Now it seems I
must think again, and treat everyone in these parts as
enemies until they are seen to be friends.'

The council agreed, and Gerrit Janszoon said, 'We lost
good men today. I heard some of the hands refer to the
place as Murderers' Bay. I suggest it be named as such on

the charts to warn future travellers.'

'Yes, unless anyone has an objection,' Abel said. 'Are there any ideas about what name we should give the land as a whole?'

'I think the name is obvious,' said Isaac Gilsemans. 'This must be part of the land found south of Tierra del Fuego, which le Maire called Staten Land.'

Visscher thought quickly. Le Maire had said Staten Land was an island, with open sea to the south. Also it was about one thousand seven hundred leagues distant, which was a long way to be sure that two lands were joined. Still it was possible—le Maire might be mistaken, and one could walk from Amsterdam to Canton, given plenty of time and strong shoes. That was a greater distance still.

'One name is as good as another,' Abel said, 'though this will be the fourth Staten Land on the charts.'

'The fourth?' asked Isaac Gilsemans. 'Which are the others?'

'After this one,' Abel said, ticking them off on his fingers, 'there's le Maire's near Cape Horn and another near the settlements in New Amsterdam.'

'And the fourth?' asked Isaac, who, in spite of his skill as a merchant and linguist, could be simple-minded at times. 'That is only three.'

'Don't forget the one with the windmills, the one we all come from,' said Abel. The others laughed.

So Staten Land it was, at least for the time. When the laughter had died, Abel continued to speak. 'The Batavia Council gave us rather confusing instructions. They could be read to mean that we were to run round the foot of the world to the coast of Chile, unless we found new land on the way. On the other hand, we were ordered to go to the longitude of the Solomon Islands, and from there look for the east coast of New Holland. But we cannot do both.'

'Could I have your reasons for this, commodore, just so that I may set them down in the record?' said Abraham Coomans.

Abel looked sharply at him. He had been suspicious of this young man for some time. 'They are simple enough, mynheer. We have neither fresh water nor fresh food. This shore looks as if it might provide both, but I am not prepared to fight to get them after what happened earlier today. It is a long way to Chile, and it would be tempting providence to go forward in that direction, hoping to find other land on the way.'

'But we are sure to have rain on the way, at least.'

'And we might have a miraculous draught of fishes to go with it, Mynheer Coomans. If they came at the same time, we would have plenty of food and drink. But we cannot rely on it.'

Francis Visscher spoke. 'The council expected too much from one voyage. I say we should go towards Tonga, and strike north from there to look for the east coast of New Holland. To try and reach Chile might be too much for us in our present state.'

'Some are prepared to face it,' said Abraham Coomans.

'None of them are seamen, I'll bet,' said Jude Tjercsen.

Abel controlled his temper, but, looking at Coomans, it was an effort. 'I've said this before, and now I will say it again. Our first task is to see that at least one ship gets back to Batavia with our results. It would be useless to find the richest land in the world if none of us return to report it. What would it have profited the King of Spain if Columbus had been lost in the Indies, and his find had never been reported in Cadiz? So now, who is in favour of looking for the shore of New Holland to the north of Tonga or the Solomons?'

Every hand was raised except that of Abraham Coomans.

As the shores of Murderers' Bay faded astern Francis said, 'You know, we could well be leaving the entrance to a strait.'

'Or the entrance to a gulf. What makes you suspect a strait?'

'A feeling I've had before, that's all. But I'm not often wrong.'

'Ah, but you have been wrong, eh?'

'I'll not deny that.'

'Then let us decide that what we are leaving is a gulf. If it is, and we tried to prove it otherwise, we could be embayed at the end of it with the westerlies and attacked by cannibals. Is your feeling strong enough to face that?'

Francis shook his head, but his eyes were wistful. 'No, all my reason tells me that we are doing the right thing.' He looked ahead under the swelling arch of the forecourse. 'We've found a fine land, though with a hostile people. And I've still got a feeling we're leaving a strait.'

It was mid summer now, south of the Line. But although they were in a corresponding latitude to that of Lisbon in the north, the weather was sometimes more like winter. They sailed north-east, trying to keep in touch with the coast, but the winds became variable and often they could not hold course. There were rain squalls which brought no relief to the thirsting ships. What water they caught was so mixed with seaspray that it was quite undrinkable.

Christmas came six days after leaving Murderers' Bay. There were live pigs in each ship brought specially for this day, and carefully fattened for the feast. On the day they were butchered there was a feast of tripe, black pudding and chitterlings. On Christmas day there was a fine smell in the ships of roast pork and sage and apple sauce—made from dried apples and a few cherished onions. Only essential work was done, and everyone had half a bottle of wine. The ships cruised close together, with all hands singing Christmas carols across the tossing waters.

The weather brightened after Christmas and the wind shifted, blowing up to almost half a gale at times. They had to shorten sail, but they made progress. Abel was worried, for the water was sinking lower in the casks. They sweetened the foul liquid by adding quicklime and straining it through charcoal, which suppressed the smell though there was still an undertaste. They masked this by adding a little arrack, so that one often heard two messmates give the old toast:

'Here's to the arrack—'

'that takes away the taste of the water!'

'And here's to the water—'

'That takes away the taste of the arrack!'

It was New Year's day 1643, and Abel was looking through some charts while reflecting on the past year. Since last August he had sailed about three thousand six hundred leagues over unknown seas and found two unknown shores. Geographers had predicted that they existed roughly where he had found them, but no seaman from Europe had ever been there. Or had they? He remembered the odd behaviour and the savagery of the Staten Landers, and their apparent knowledge of the effect of gunfire. Still he hoped he would be the first to report these lands. He was astonished at the distance he had sailed since August. Yes, 1642 had been a wonderful year.

This inward satisfaction was flawed by the reality of their present situation. A sudden storm, an outward thrust of the coast, a hidden shoal—any of these things could bring all his efforts to nothing. If Batavia did not learn of his discoveries, all the time and money spent making them would be wasted. They were far from home and could not go on much farther without water and fresh food.

On 4th January the coast they had been following northwards for a hundred and fifty leagues turned east, and a group of islands showed to the north. On the chart they were making, the cape on the mainland was named Cape Maria van Diemen, in honour of the governor's wife, and others were named the Three Kings Islands. This was not because there were three islands, but because they were sighted on the feast of that name.

Through the telescope Francis observed a white streak marking one of the cliffs. 'Have a look at that, commodore,' he said, handing over the glass. 'I think it's a waterfall.'

'Or bird droppings, like those we saw on the cliffs in Van Diemen's Land,' Abel replied. 'However, it's worth a look. And if it is water, pray that there's nothing to prevent us getting to it.'

They drew closer. It was water, a bright fall gushing from the cliff. Francis took a boat as close inshore as possible, but he could make no landing at that point. The sea thundered against the foot of the cliffs and the breakers burst on the reefs with a fearful noise. Next day he went in again with Isaac Gilsemans. They took both longboats, each towing a string of empty water casks. Reaching the inaccessible spring, they turned along the shore to find other water or an easier landing. They found neither. Two men appeared, well armed, looking exactly like those at Murderers' Bay. They passed surefooted over the craggy ground, their shouts bringing others running swiftly to the scene. Their weapons were wooden maces and stone-headed axes, and every so often some of them danced a terrifying war dance, leaving no doubt as to their intentions.

They did not seem to have canoes, or perhaps they thought it was too rough to launch them. There was no safe landing in this place, and presently Isaac and Francis came in sight of the waterfall again. The parched throats of the seamen ached at the sight and sound of it, but to land on this island would be impossible, for none of the Dutchmen would escape alive. So, with regret, they drew away from the new Staten Land, since what little had been seen of it suggested it might be a good land to live in.

'That would seem to settle it,' Abel said to Francis, as the long line of cliff astern sank below the horizon. 'Whatever land that is, it is not part of New Holland.' His eyes ran across the tossing sea. 'All this water, and none of it fit to drink! What did you say the nearest certain land was, Francis?'

'The Tonga Islands, I think. Jacob le Maire charted them thirty years ago.'

'Le Maire again? We seem to be treading on his heels a good deal on this voyage.'

'Except he came from the east and we from the west. If two men start on the same road from opposite ends, it is likely they will meet in the middle.'

'True enough! What position do you have for Tonga?'

'I have 20° south and about 195° east of Madeira. Of course, neither may be quite correct. I expect the latitude is pretty well right, though.'

'And the old trouble with longitude, eh? When we raise Tonga, we'll try and fix it properly with a round of lunar sights. What would you suggest as a course?'

'The very simplest—north to 20° latitude, then run the easting down.'

6

Return to Batavia

WHEN they sighted Tonga on 19th January, there was a general feeling of relief to be in a known world again.

They made a landing two days later, and the golden-skinned islanders were welcoming and friendly. The council was relieved, for le Maire had met trouble on some of the islands in Tonga. Abel was especially glad of the friend-liness, for he had to have fresh water. The ration had been cut to two litres a day, and rationing water was a bad thing to do. Of course, no seaman could be allowed unlimited water at sea, but two litres was not sufficient for a man doing hard work in hot weather. So far the crew had borne with it, but it was as well not to strain them too far; Abel knew there was always the threat of mutiny to bear in mind.

With a supply of water the rest of the voyage should be a pleasant one. Once more they were in the tropics and having flying-fish weather. The first fresh food any of them had seen in weeks were some of these flying-fish, caught by a flaw of wind and blown on board. Broiled, they made tasty eating, though many of the men were so avid for fresh food that they peeled off the head, fins and guts and ate the fish raw!

When Schouten and le Maire had discovered Tonga in 1616, the ships had been attacked, so Abel approached the lagoon at Tongatabu with his boarding-nets rigged and the swivels loaded. The islanders, however, met them in friend-ship, although they proved to be great thieves.

It took some time to arrange for the filling of the water-casks, since at first they had no speech in common. Isaac

Gilsemans said he thought that some words the Tongans used were the same as those he had heard from the warriors of Staten Land, but since they could not comprehend that either, this was no help. Before the flotilla left, however, there was understanding between them, and a phrasebook that would assist future travellers. No one on the ships went thirsty during this time, for the islanders provided quantities of coconuts, green in the husk and full of delicious liquid that would have hardened into the kernel as the nuts ripened.

While the discussions were going on about water, the ship was never free of visitors. Each came with a gift—fish, yams, bananas, even small pigs—expecting to be given cloth or iron in return. In spite of this, they tried to steal anything they could lay their hands on.

'I never knew such thieves,' said Isaac Gilsemans. 'This morning one of them was making off with a spare link of anchor chain.'

'And you asked for it back, I hope,' said Abel.

'To be sure I did!'

'And it was returned?'

'Quite willingly.'

'What the man did was not theft as we judge it; he did not want it for himself. There are people like this in Borneo, who hold everything in common. No single person owns even a fish-hook. Everything belongs to the village. The Tongans must be the same; everything belongs to all, and they are not stealing but borrowing. Sometimes it's only curiosity, and they take a thing because it catches their eye.'

Francis Visscher had joined them and listened to the last part of the conversation. 'I can understand them borrowing,' he said, 'if they know the use of the things they take. But what about one of them in my cabin, calmly "borrowing" my instruments?'

'They are like children in some ways, Francis. Don't children often want to handle and play with things they don't understand?'

'You really don't think they are thieves, commodore?'

'Not in our sense, though I admit what they do some-times has the same effect. We need to keep on friendly terms with them, so I'll make an order that all valuables are stowed under lock and key. And another, that even in cases of apparent theft, we keep on good terms with the Tongans. We don't want to stir up a hornet's nest for future travellers.'

Isaac smiled. 'Not even if they are Spaniards?'

'Not even then. We are far enough from Holland to regard all men as brothers. It will be a sad day for the world when we enlist people like these Tongans to aid us in our wars in Europe.'

It took six days to arrange to fill the water-casks, and a further six to do it. Lugging the filled casks over the soft ground was hard work, and four filled casks in a day was good going. But the change of occupation, with unlimited fresh food and water, put new heart into the men, and Abel's fears of a possible mutiny over rations died down.

Then another issue arose. It was in connection with the island women. The council could not decide whether the women, too, were common property, or whether they were free to bestow their favours where they wished.

'I cannot decide whether they even marry,' said Abel.

'I suppose they do,' said Jude Tjercsen. 'There are cer-tainly plenty of children.'

'Yes, but have you noticed they play together in age-groups? You never see a family party. I wish I spoke the language, to find out their way of life.'

'I've noticed our men—even some of the anchor watch —are slipping ashore at night. It can only be the women that attract them,' said Isaac Gilsemans.

'What can you expect, after five months at sea? There was nothing for them at Mauritius,' Gerrit Janszoon spoke out.

Abel understood the intoxication of being in a foreign port, and the feeling that whatever one did was of little moment, since the ship would sail in a few days' time and might never return. But in spite of his orders men slipped ashore in the anchor watch, and he had to order a flogging for two of the culprits.

Abel did not like flogging, but discipline had to be preserved. Stopping a man's pay was no punishment, since none of them would be paid in money until the ship reached Batavia. By that time the reason for the punishment would be forgotten. Nor was the ordering of extra work practical. The men already worked watch-and-watch at sea, four hours on and four off, seven days a week, and there was a limit to what they could stand. But the floggings were few and the stripes laid on lightly; the greatest wound was to the victim's pride. There was no point in crippling a man with the lash, as the English and the Spanish were said to do. That would only mean his share of work would have to be done by others.

Pleased as he had been to arrive at Tonga, Abel was almost as pleased to leave. Life seemed happy enough on the island, but he could not rid his mind of the thought that the Tongans might be cannibals like the men of Murderers' Bay. Although there was no direct evidence of cannibalism, none of the officers felt entirely comfortable when they were alone among a group of Tongans.

It was now the monsoon season, and Abel did not know what wind and weather would be like in these parts. He summoned a council to discuss what direction they should take and was pleased with the decision, which was the one he would have made himself. It was agreed that they should sail north and then west towards Batavia, keeping a lookout for the east coast of New Holland, or the coast of New Guinea. Charts of New Guinea were greatly needed.

After leaving Tonga they ran into monsoon weather with overcast skies and dense mists at night. Moulds grew on wood and leather, and there was a faint smell of decay through the ships. For six weeks they scarcely saw either sun or stars, and all navigation was by dead reckoning. It was not until the middle of March that the sky cleared long enough to enable them to fix their latitude. After navigating so long by guess, Abel was surprised that he and Francis were only twenty-three leagues out in their reckoning. With no charted land to give them a new point of departure, this was a great achievement.

They found more new land on 22nd March, and for three days they sailed through a sea strewn with coral reefs. Sometimes boats had to be manned to tow the ships clear of the rocks, while the crew on board trimmed and re-trimmed the sails to take advantage of the wind.

The captains and mates conned the ships through the channels from the foremast-head, shouting the steering orders down to the quartermaster at the whipstaff. On one such day Francis said to Abel, 'It would be a good thing on such a voyage as this to have a much smaller ship, shallow-drafted like a galliot, to go ahead sounding a channel for the others.'

'I'll bear it in mind,' said Abel, red-eyed from lack of sleep, 'and recommend it to the governor. Only it won't be me who will command it—one such voyage is enough for a lifetime!'

On 25th March they had a visit from a canoe crewed by three men. These men were darker than any the Dutchmen had ever seen, and the canoe was badly made and ill-kept. These newcomers had no use for iron, but they readily traded coconuts for beads. There was little wind that day, and soon the ships were surrounded by dozens of canoes. Beads for exchange began to run low, and the men in the canoes became threatening while a new keg was being broken out from the hold. Whether the Dutch ships would have been attacked or not was doubtful, for a strong breeze blew up, and they moved off leaving the canoes behind. They sailed clear of the reefs, but not into open water, since there was always one or two islands within sight.

At the end of March they were again approached by two canoes. These were small and roughly made, with a trimmed log attached to either side as outriggers. They were crewed by nine very small black men, who showed no fear at the sight of the ships. One made a peace sign by breaking an arrow, sticking the headed end in his mop of hair and holding out the feathered end towards the ships. They exchanged gifts with these friendly people, parted on good terms with them, and hoped that their meeting had been a good omen. For on the same day they sighted a coast that just might be the eastern shore of New Holland. Behind the coast were mountains, stretching north-west and south-east far into the distance.

Then Francis recognized Cape St Maria from a drawing on a chart by de Quiros, and their optimism died. They realized this was not the coast of New Holland, but an outlying island to the north of New Guinea, and the islands they had sailed through must have been the elusive Solomons.

But just to find something on a chart made them feel they were nearing home, even though Batavia lay seven hundred leagues away, with the whole of New Guinea in between. De Torres had sailed through a strait between New Guinea and New Holland, but since he was the only one to find this strait, few believed in it. These days the Portuguese were best known to the Dutch as lackeys of Spain, and their credit in maritime matters had slipped a long way since the days of Vasco da Gama. Abel would have to round the northern tip of New Guinea to get home, and it was unclear from the various charts just where this was. But Schouten and le Maire, both good Dutchmen, had rounded it, so it was there all right.

Once clear of New Guinea, Abel could expect to meet ships in the Timor and Ambon trade. He might even meet Gerrit Demmer, his old shipmate, whom he had last heard of in these parts. Anyway, it would be good to sail in known waters again and meet a friendly ship.

In the middle of April they experienced an earthquake at

sea, the first any of them had known. It was as if the sea-bed had reared and struck the keel a violent blow. Abel rushed on deck, but there was little to be seen, because it was just before sunrise. There was a stench of sulphur and decay, and as it grew light they saw the sea was strewn with dead marine life. While the Javanese burned incense and struck gongs to asuage the spirits of the deep, the Dutch gave thanks to God for their lives and netted the edible fish and broiled them for breakfast.

They cruised among islands which had been reported either by Schouten, le Maire or de Torres. Reconciling the different charts was largely an act of faith. The volcano, named Vulcanus,* which le Maire had placed on the mainland, proved to be on an island. There was no doubt about it, for the great pulsing fire was visible for miles.

One day towards the end of April they anchored about a league from the Schouten Islands, one of the two groups discovered by that captain and named after him on the chart. They were hopeful of being able to talk to the islanders because they had studied a wordbook made by Schouten himself. They were not short of water, but fresh food was always welcome. Next day they met the islanders, and found that they could, indeed, make themselves understood. The health of Captain Schouten was drunk that night in gratitude for the help his wordbook had given them in obtaining yams and limes from the islanders.

The people of this place all seemed to be old. They were very small in stature and dark-skinned, wearing nothing but breech-clouts of bark cloth. Even so, it was difficult to tell the men from the women. They were quarrelsome, too, and quick to take up their weapons. An argument arose one day, and a seaman was shot by an arrow through the thick of the thigh. Tempers ran high among the man's messmates, and the officers had to use the flat of their swords to keep order.

'An accident, my boy,' said Abel as he dressed the wound,

* Karkar Island, near Astrolabe Bay.

93

'and think yourself lucky it was the leg and not your neck.'

'I won't be poisoned with it?'

'Poisoned! After all the good arrack I've swabbed it with? Not on your life! By the time we get to Batavia your girl won't even be able to see the scar.'

All the same Abel dressed the wound every day, and was very glad when it healed. For he too had wondered about poison.

They found Schouten's second island, called Biak, with its spine of hills and outlying fangs of coral. The people here were the same as those farther down the coast.

The second week in May they met a fleet of fishing canoes, well-made craft shining and polished with coconut oil. Some of the fishermen could speak Dutch since they were Ternatese, and their rajah was an ally of the company. Just to hear strangers speaking Dutch made Abel feel nearer home.

The next week they arrived in Gilolo. Abel had never been there before, though the place was famous in the Indies. Some trick of the ocean caused a current that piled the beaches high with driftwood, and it was said that every fallen tree in the Indies ended up there.

Early in June they met two junks which proved to be friendly. There were many pirate junks in these waters, and the flotilla showed itself ready for action, with nettings rigged and the gun-ports open. The serangs of the junks sculled over in sampans to show their passports and bring welcome sacks of Chinese cabbage, for they were only two days out from Batavia.

The flotilla arrived home on 15th June 1643, ten months and one day after setting out. The news of the return flashed quickly round the port, and a boat came out to meet them with the governor, Jannetie, Claesgen and Mevrouw Visscher on board. There was talk and laughter in the great cabin of the *Heemskerck* that night, and a feast of fresh food. Happy singing as the wine went round could be heard until the rising sun dimmed the light of the silver hanging-lamps.

Explorer in Doubt: 1644

1

The Batavia Council

'Y O U ' V E served on the council before,' the governor said to Abel, 'so you should know something about it. Most members are merchants who are not acquainted with the sea. The first time many of them set foot on a deck was when they came out, and the next time will be when they go back.'

'Merchants seem to learn little of the sea,' said Abel, 'but the seamen cannot help learning about trade. There should be more of us on the council who are familiar with both aspects.'

'And if there were more seamen sitting round the table, who would be out earning the profit for the company?'

'That's what I said,' stated Francis Visscher. 'In time, any council becomes an assembly of counting-house men and lawyers. Men who can do business while staying in one place, joined occasionally by those like you, Abel, just temporarily and for a special purpose. The only seamen permanently on the council are elderly men who have retired from a life at sea.'

'But it is the merchant members who will judge our voyage,' said Abel angrily.

'Patience, Abel! The council will report to The Hague, but there is nothing in the constitution to say I cannot make a separate report of my own. And I am—or was—a seaman, and you can rest assured that I will make fair comment.'

'Tell me this, mynheer, what would you have done in my place?'

'Exactly as you have done—sailed with prudence rather

than dash, and reported here with my findings. There is plenty of time for later voyages to fill in the outline of your discoveries. But about this council, will you take a word of advice?'

'Well, I will listen to it.'

'Abel, Francis was your pilot-major, so let him submit the report. You and I understand one another, but you are too forthright to make a good man for the council.'

'Too quick-tempered, you mean? Well, you may be right. I find it easier to deal with Javanese seamen than merchants of my own kind.' He turned to the pilot. 'Francis, you and I are a good team. I think I'm the better seaman, but you are a better draughtsman. Speak to the council by all means, but when you do, speak for all who were with us in the ships, from the skippers to the cookboys. And speak especially for those poor souls we buried off Murderers' Bay.'

The council usually met on Fridays, but there was a special session on 18th June to receive the report of the voyage. At eight in the morning Abel and Francis attended the Council House overlooking the roadstead to Smits Island. It was a view that reflected the growing power of the company. Ships of every European nation—except Spain— were anchored there alongside rakish dhows and square-cut Chinese junks. Few ports in the world could show such a variety of shipping or such valuable trade.

Francis was thoughtful as they waited in an ante-chamber to be summoned before the council. It was no wonder, he thought, that governors of the company were dazzled by wealth. Gold was the medium they dealt with, as sailors dealt with the sea. Merchants were, therefore, bound to have different values, since their medium was permanent and indestructible, while the sea was inconstant. The sea-man lived for the present but the merchant could plan for the future.

Special session or not, there was always other business

to occupy the council. The two explorers were kept waiting for so long that it seemed to them a deliberate indication that the voyage was only of minor importance. Abel had the impression that as soon as the ships were over the horizon, the council had forgotten them. He mentioned this to Francis.

'You might well be right,' said the pilot, 'but it's only what we do ourselves. I can't remember we talked much of the council when we were sailing eastward in the Southern Ocean.'

It was almost noon when, at last, they went into the council. But they found Gilsemans and Coomans had already made their report. Isaac Gilsemans was looking uncomfortable, but Coomans was looking very smug.

The governor spoke first, with Abel's official journal in front of him. 'This is an account of a ten-month voyage of exploration. It satisfies me, for it is very complete. There is only one thing, decisions are mentioned, but not always the reasons for making them.'

Adam van der Post, a stout middle-aged man, spoke. 'I have a question. What was the profit on this voyage, and what was brought here in the way of trade?'

Visscher's voice was calm. 'There was no profit, and we brought nothing back except a few quintals of pearlshell from Tonga.'

A murmur ran round the table, of confirmation rather than surprise. Abel recalled that the merchants had already reported.

'That is the only trade you made in a ten-month voyage?' asked Nicholas Schaeffer.

'That is all, mynheer. But you will remember that this voyage was one of exploration, seeking markets for future rather than for present profit.'

'Seeking new markets will be the ruin of the company,' said van der Post. 'Why can't we be content with what we have?'

'I will answer that,' said the governor. 'A company such

99

as ours is conceived and born, it has its infancy and growth, it matures, declines and dies. Once it ceases to grow, in fact, it begins to die, though the dying may take a long time.'

Van der Post made an impatient noise. 'And at what stage are we now?' he asked.

'Barely out of infancy, mynheer, and still growing. Voyages such as Commodore Tasman's are our growing pains, and will not happen in our maturity.'

Nicholas Schaeffer also uttered an impatient noise. 'Hmph, mynheer!' he grunted. 'I took you for a man of good Dutch common sense. Under good management there is no reason why this company should not go on for ever.'

'Nothing lasts for ever, Mynheer Schaeffer—nothing! Though it is true that some things appear to. There are people who have died in their middle age, to whom the Spanish Wars must seem to have lasted for ever. But there are old men alive who saw their beginning, and young men who will see their end. For ever, to the ordinary man, merely means to extend beyond an average lifetime.'

'I agree with that,' said Piet Grobler, a slender man in his forties. 'But how long do you think a company like this will last?'

'Long after you and I are forgotten. Maybe about two hundred years. Men come and go, guilds and companies come and go, cities and nations come and go. It is a law of nature.' He mopped his brow with a batik kerchief. 'But we are not getting on with the business of the day. Have we finished discussing trade? Or are there any questions?'

Adriaan Doorman, the port-captain from Onrust, spoke. 'I'd like to know how much land this voyage discovered, and the route sailed.'

'I will do my best to tell you everything,' said Francis. 'We looked for Captain Keeling's islands on the way to Mauritius, and also Diego Ruys island, but saw no sign of either. Then we left Fort Frederik Hendrik on 7th October last year and steered south-east. By the 22nd of the month we were in 38° south, and had entered the region of the westerly winds. We altered course to the east-south-east and reached our farthest south at 49°04′ on 7th November. Then we decided to turn to the north.'

'Why, mynheer? Schouten and le Maire pressed farther south than that.'

'We turned because we were afraid of seas and weather. Had we found a coast in that region, we would never have been able to claw away from it.'

'So, please go on.'

'We altered course to east-south-east, by and large, until we found a land in latitude 42° south, which we named for the governor.'

'It might have been more fitting to name it for the company,' said van der Post.

'In naming it for the governor, we also honoured the company,' said Francis diplomatically, 'but it was the governor who gave us our orders.'

'And how long did you stay in this new land?'

'Until 6th December, captain.'

'And in that time you could not tell whether this land was island or mainland? Or so you say in the journal.' It was van der Post speaking again.

'There are times when only a bird can tell that, mynheer. It is not easily decided beating up a strange shore against contrary winds.'

There was a rumble of laughter at this, in which the merchant did not join. But he said, 'And how far did you trace this new coast you say you found?'

Abel sprang to his feet. 'If I say I found a coast, then there was a coast to be found. Do you imply that I lied in my journal?'

'No, no, by all means! But you might be mistaken.'

The governor hastened to make peace. 'Mynheer van der Post, there can be no doubt about the existence of this land bearing my name. The commodore and the pilot-major are both good navigators, or I would not have sent them on this voyage. I'd stake my head on the accuracy of their latitude, though I agree that longitude is a difficult quantity to arrive at.' He turned to Visscher. 'Tell the council—for those who have not read the journal—how far you followed this coast.'

'More than ninety leagues, your excellency. First to the south-east then east, and finally north-east, charting it as we went.'

'And you made landings?' asked Captain Doorman.

'We made three, though one of them was by a single man. Peter Jacobs, the carpenter, swam ashore through the surf with a line round his waist.'

There was a murmur of surprise. 'Why was this?' asked the port-captain.

'To claim the land in the name of the States-General of the United Provinces of the Netherlands and the company. He towed ashore a stake and a lead tablet, and set them up beyond high-tide mark. It should be there for a long time.'

'Why the States-General, commodore? Surely the company will live the longer.'

There was a laugh at this, and Abel said, 'Mynheer, one will certainly outlast the other, but I don't know which it will be. I saw no harm in claiming the land in both names.'

'Why didn't you follow this coast to find out whether it was part of New Holland?' asked Captain Doorman.

'I wish I had now,' said Abel, 'but that is hindsight. Because of the wind we had trouble keeping in touch with the coast. I was concerned about fresh water, so I decided to make for Tonga and the Solomons and to find the coast of New Holland from there.'

'And you found more new land on the way?'

'Yes, they did!' said Nicholas Schaeffer. 'They stirred up a hornet's nest of trouble and lost a dozen men!'

'We stirred up no trouble. We were attacked. And we lost four men, not twelve.'

'You allowed four men to be killed by naked savages?'

Abel wiped his brow. How could he make this pot-bellied

merchant see what it had been like? 'These people were not naked savages. Some wore garments of cloth, and their canoes were large and well built. I did not *allow* four men to be killed. On the contrary, I took careful steps to avoid loss of life by either parties. It was my policy throughout this voyage to treat all men as friends until they proved to be otherwise. These people were suspicious of us, and I made no gesture to alarm them.'

'They were suspicious of you, just as we would be of strange ships approaching these shores,' said the governor.

'Exactly! We are the first to report this coast, but are we the first from Europe to visit it? Suppose a Spanish ship had been there before us, and behaved towards these people as they did to the West Indians, with a sword in one hand and a crucifix in the other. They cannot be expected to tell Dutch from Spaniard.'

'If I may say so, that is a rather soft-hearted view,' said Captain Doorman.

'I could take offence at that, captain, but consider the facts. These people appeared to have knowledge of gunfire, for never once did they come within range of our swivels. They steered from side to side as they pulled away, which you know to be the best way of avoiding shot. And if they have been wronged by others, it will take time for us to win their confidence.'

'That is most interesting,' said the governor. 'You do not mention this in your journal?'

'No, it is a matter of conjecture and a journal entry should be a matter of fact.'

'That's true enough,' said the port-captain. 'Have you thought of a way of winning their friendship?'

'We have a glimmering of a plan. Their language sounds similar to that of the Tongans. When we know the Tongans better, and can speak their language, we might be able to communicate with the Staten Landers.'

'Very promising!' said the governor. 'Though I don't know when we will be able to try it out. I'd have done just the same in your place: pulled out and thought about the next step. Let's hope one day we can change the name of Murderers' Bay, but meanwhile we'll let it stand as a reminder. Now what was your next step?'

The meeting went on all day, and long shadows were slanting through the palms as Abel went home. Jannetie greeted him with a jug of punch and words of comfort.

'No need to tell me what was said,' she remarked, as she poured him a drink. 'Don't forget, I hear the wives at the sewing circle at the predikant's house every Tuesday. Merchants! They think of nothing but profit.'

'Quite rightly,' said Abel, as a servant drew off his buckled shoes and he put on his house shoes. 'Profit is the life-blood of a company and some day it will be made from my discoveries.' He took a draught of his punch and laughed. 'But it might be a long time before we see it.'

'I *know* you are right, my love. I know it! You and the governor will be remembered long after these merchants are forgotten!'

It was approaching Christmas before the council's report on the voyage was sent off to The Hague, and when Abel and Francis saw it they were appalled. Nothing that Abel had done was considered right. He had not found out the extent of his discoveries, he had not sailed to Chile, and he had not found the east coast of New Holland.

'If that's accepted in The Hague,' he said, 'it's the finish of me with the company. I might as well take Francis and go back to Holland and the herring fishery.'

The governor clapped him on the shoulder. 'Cheer up, Abel! That report won't be accepted—or if it is, I'll sign on in the herring fleet with you. Think of Columbus!'

'What's he got to do with it?'

'He made four voyages to the New World, yet never set foot on the mainland.'

'Well?'

'If he'd set out to discover the extent of his discoveries, he would have been about a hundred and eighty by now— and the task still unfinished. So cheer up. I and the seamen on the council sent in another report, upholding you in every way.'

'A minority report.'

'Ah, but it will carry more weight than twenty reports made by merchants. Incidentally, not all the merchants were against you. Mynheer Gilsemans refused to sign the council report.'

'I'll wager Coomans did!'

'As a matter of fact, he did, but he's the council's lackey. He'll pander to any merchant higher in status than himself, and kick anyone in the face who is beneath him. But never mind Coomans while Gilsemans is your friend.' The governor shuffled in a drawer and found a sheaf of papers tied with a tape. 'And now, forget all about it. Go and see Francis and look these papers over.'

'What are they?'

'Plans for another voyage.'

'Not to find a new way to Chile?'

'No, quite the opposite direction. Luiz de Torres claimed there was a strait between New Guinea and New Holland. If there is, it would be a way to discover New Holland's east coast. I'd like you to go and take a look.'

2

New Guinea Landing

'OF course,' said the governor, after the ladies had withdrawn to the parlour for coffee and pipes had been lit
round the dining-table, 'some of the merchants are crazy
about the idea of trade with Chile. As if the Spaniards
would allow us to get a footing in those parts.'

It was early in January 1644, and Abel and Francis were
dining with the governor.

'But you said we were not to look for the Chile passage
in this new voyage,' stated Abel.

'And I meant it. Unless the council at The Hague change
their minds, no ship of this company will ever travel
towards South America again.'

'Why is that, mynheer?' asked Francis.

'For two reasons. There is little point in looking for a
new way to Europe when we already have a proved route
by way of Mauritius. Especially if we set up another station
at the Cape of Good Hope.'

'Now, that would be a splendid idea! We could fix its
longitude, and use it as a fresh departure point.'

'More to the point, we could grow vegetables and run
beef cattle there. But there's another reason why you will
not be seeking Chile, and that's the Dutch *West* Indies
Company, of New Amsterdam and St Eustace. Their
charter gives them a right to trade over all the Americas,
from Cape Horn to the Arctic.'

'The east and the west coasts?'

'Yes, and the north-west passage, if they can find it. So
that settles that.'

'What about sending us to Van Diemen's Land again?'

'Certainly, provided you approach it by Torres's strait and the east coast of New Holland.'

The new expedition was to consist of three ships. *Limmen*, a sister ship to *Heemskerck*, *Zeemeeuw*, sister ship to *Zeehaen*, and *Bracq*. The third was a galliot of only twenty tonnes, able to proceed under sail or sweeps. She would be uncomfortable in heavy seas, but the burden on her crew could be eased by frequent changes with the other ships. Abel and Francis were delighted with her.

'She's a good one,' said Abel, as he looked over the squat hull and massive leeboards. Galliots were designed for in-shore work off the Dutch coast. They sat upright on the sands as the tide fell, and proceeded under sweeps if the wind failed. There were families in the Netherlands who spent all their lives in such craft.

'Only she'll be slow on a sea passage,' said Francis.

'We'll have her rerigged. She's been used as a harbour craft, so her sail has been cut down. I'll have the jib-boom refitted, so that she can carry more headsail, and balance it with a mizen rigged forward of the tiller. With a beam wind she'll have the heels of all of us.'

'Well, it's good we've got her, but it's a pity we have to go to Makassar and Ambon before we look for a strait. We'll miss some good sailing weather.'

'Be thankful we're going at all, Francis. I think the governor arranged these two outward calls on purpose. If anything goes wrong, and at sea something almost always does, Makassar and Ambon can take some of the blame.' He poured out two glasses of arrack and added lime juice, his eyes twinkling as he held one out to his friend. 'Here's to honest trade!'

The flotilla left Batavia at the end of January 1644. They did not know it, but this was to be a great year in the history of the Netherlands. The English king had been defeated by his parliament in battle, which meant that Spanish arms, men, and gold could no longer be landed in west England and re-embark on the east coast for a quick passage across the Narrow Seas to the Netherlands. So Admiral Tromp was reaping a rich harvest from Spanish argosies in the English Channel, while Prince Frederik Hendrik singed Spanish beards by capturing the *Sas van Ghent*. The end of the Eighty Years' War was in sight.

It was flattering, thought Abel, that so many of the men who had sailed with him on the previous voyage were willing to sign on with him again. Mynheer Coomans was not one of them, which was no surprise, and his place had been taken by Anthony Blauw. Dirk Haen, skipper of the *Zeemeeuw*, was another new face, as was Jasper Koos of the *Bracq*. There were nine on the Commodore's Council this voyage, and six had sailed with him before. For the first month they sailed in convoy with other company ships, shortening sail at sunset so that passengers would be disturbed as little as possible by noise on deck during the night. Land was rarely out of sight, and the pilots always knew where they were.

They came to Makassar on 22nd February with a land breeze bringing the perfume of spices and flowers out to the ships. They stayed two days, setting the merchant Adriaan van Zuydwyck ashore and taking on fresh water and vegetables. Then they left for Ambon.

They arrived in mid afternoon, and Abel went ashore to pay his official calls. It was nine years since he had last been to Ambon, and it had changed a great deal. There were now stone buildings along the waterfront, where previously there had only been bamboo-and-thatch ones.

At the residence Abel made his formal bow to the governor, a tall, sallow-faced man wearing spectacles. 'Allow me to introduce myself, excellency. Commodore Abel Tasman, of the ships *Limmen* and *Zeemeeuw* and the galliot *Bracq*. May I—' He broke off suddenly, for something in the governor's face shook his memory. Stepping forward, Abel stretched out his hand. 'Gerrit Demmer, my old shipmate! Who would have thought to meet you here?'

It was, unbelievably, Gerrit Demmer, who had stood by him at his second marriage, hauled on the same ropes, and tramped to The Hague with him when they first served with the company. It was the spectacles, of course, that had fooled him. Gerrit had always been bothered by poor sight, and Abel vaguely remembered he had transferred from the marine to the administrative side of the company.

It was impossible to talk of all the doings of the past nine years in one or even two days, and Gerrit decided to take a passage with the flotilla to Banda. This was to be the point of departure for New Guinea, so that if the ships were late in returning, a search party would know where to begin looking. Gerrit and Margrethe Demmer would return to Ambon in a country ship.

'I'm really combining business with pleasure,' said Gerrit. 'I need to see Cornelius Witsen, the factor at Banda, and yours will probably be the most comfortable ship going that way for months. One gets plenty of travel in these parts in native trading boats stinking of stale fish.'

It is forty leagues from Ambon to Banda, and the trip took five days. They had good weather for it, with a cooling shower early afternoon every day. The nights were warm, and the seas glowed with green fire as the ships clove the water. On the third night out, the conversation turned to the aims of the present voyage. It was a gentle evening, with only a slight breeze on deck as they sat in the glow of the glass-shielded candles.

'I sometimes wish I were at sea again,' said Gerrit, lighting his pipe. 'Think of it! Not a mosquito for leagues.'

'It's not always like this, old friend.'

'Oh, I know. I can recall other ships in colder seas. But to be at sea on a night like this, having eaten a good supper, and your pipe drawing well—it's as near heaven as a man will get on this earth.'

'Yet there are hellish enough spots not so very far away.'

'So I understand. But tell me, where do you go from Banda?'

Mock quoting from his orders, Abel droned in a sing-song voice, 'You will proceed to the New Guinea coast, and in eight degrees south look for the strait reported by Luiz de Torres.' Francis Visscher took up the strain as he stopped for breath.

'Finding it, you will then seek the east coast of New Holland—'

'And discover whether that links up with Van Diemen's Land—'

'Or Staten Land—'

'But if there is no strait—'

'You will turn westward and follow the north coast of New Holland—'

'If there is such a thing—'

'To seventeen degrees south,' Abel paused and grinned at Francis, then continued in his normal voice. 'That's about all, except to leave messages in every prominent place before going back to Batavia through Sunda Strait.'

Gerrit whistled. 'A tall order! But at least you know the Sunda Strait.'

'Yes, that's always something.'

'How long are you victualled for?'

'Eight months. We hope to spin that out a bit, of course. It all depends on what kind of country we find, and what grows there.'

Gerrit shook his head. 'I don't fancy your chances of trading for food. I've been at Ambon for three years, which is as close as any civilized place to New Guinea. As far as finding victuals, you might just as easily end up in a cooking-pot yourself.'

'We're well armed,' said Francis, 'and we've been before. We'll take no chances.'

'Torres's strait?' said Gerrit, changing the subject. 'Most seamen don't believe it exists.'

'And if it does, we are searching for it from the wrong end,' said Francis. 'But orders are orders!'

'The wrong end. Why do you say that?'

'Because from this end we shall have the south-east trades dead foul, to sail a sea that is said to be half coral and half water. And while coral is soft enough, as rocks go, it can tear the bottom out of a ship as well as any.'

'You have said all this to the Batavia Council, I presume?'

'Over and over again, Gerrit. Over and over again. But if we were to come at all, we had to do it this way, to fit in with the trading programme. And who knows? We may be lucky and find the strait.'

'You really seem to care for this work, Abel.'

'Care for it? I suppose I do. Yes, ever since I was a lad, I've enjoyed a new landfall.'

'And all the more if you were first to see it! Yes you always were one for seeing over the far side of the hill. It's just as well for the company that there are a few like you, but as far as I'm concerned, I'll settle for trade!'

On arrival at Banda they met the factor, Cornelius Witsen. 'So you are bound for New Guinea, commodore? Maybe I can help you. There's a seaman here, Jan Jorissen, who was castaway in New Guinea for two years after the wreck of the *Ritter*. For some reason—he thinks it was because he has red hair—he was the only one not killed. He learnt the language in New Guinea, and could go with you as an interpreter.'

Something made Abel suspicious of the offer. 'Is this Jorissen willing to go?'

'I think he'd be glad to get away. In fact, he is mixed up in some trouble with a woman here, and he is not the marrying kind.'

Abel smiled. 'There are many who go to sea for that reason. I'll sign him on to save him from a jealous father's parang. Or is it a jealous husband?'

It was a leap year in 1644, and they left Banda on 29th February. Half the population farewelled them in surfboats, turning back only when the land had almost faded from sight. Under full sail, the flotilla set out on the long beat against the trade winds for the coast of New Guinea, two

hundred leagues away. With adverse winds they had to
make long tacks to achieve any headway in the right
direction. Sometimes the sails were set and the yards
braced twice in a watch, and here the *Bracq* had the best of
it. Her fore-and-aft rig made her handier in a beam wind.

On 12th March a dark line on the horizon could only
mean land. The sea was so shallow and clear that sometimes
the bottom could be seen from on deck, and constant
soundings were taken with the lead and line.

'By the mark, four!' called the leadsman. Abel looked
calm, but four fathoms was only twice what the ship drew.

'What is on the bottom?' he asked.

The leadsman rubbed his thumb over the tallow arming
of the lead. 'Sand and broken shell.'

'Anchor, if you please, Francis.' Abel now passed on his
orders easily in the form of requests, but in earlier voyages
he had often forgotten he was commodore and given them
direct. 'Hand over the ship to the mate, and warn Jorissen
the interpreter. We'll go ashore in the *Bracq*.'

'You've changed your mind about leading shore
expeditions?'

'I have an official second in command this voyage—Dirk
Haen. He can do the waiting while I savour the adventure.'

'And how many shall we take?'

'Six marines and their officer, two gunners' mates and
the longboats crew, the seamen armed with cutlasses and
the marines with their muskets.'

Bracq swept towards the low shore, her great mainsail
swelling in the light breeze. There were frequent changes
of course, but this was no problem to a small ship with, in
effect, a double crew. All were eager to get ashore, and
even the marines hauled eagerly on sheets and halliards as
required. Astride the bowsprit, a seaman measured the
depth with a two-fathom pole.

Three hours later, with the shore still half a mile distant,
a leeboard scraped over a sandbank, stirring a muddy cloud
from the water.

Jasper Koos ran to the seaman with the sounding-pole. 'What depth?' he asked.

'By the deep, a fathom, skipper.'

'Let go the anchor and strike all sail!' Then to the leadsman he said, 'Take the five-minute glass and make a sounding at every turn, to give us an idea of the run of the tide.'

'Yes, skipper! Sound every five minutes and keep a tally.'

Limmen's longboat was towing astern and the gunners' mate fitted a swivel at the bow as the crew dropped into it. They brought a chest with half a dozen spare loaded breechblocks. The marines sat on the thwarts with lengths of burning slowmatch looped through their hatbands. This would be no second Murderers' Bay if Abel could help it!

It was hotter inshore than it had been at sea, and the rowers' shirts were dark with sweat. The offshore breeze brought a swamp stench with it, as well as thousands of insects.

They grounded some distance from the water's edge, which meant that the beach was out of range of the swivel gun. Well, Abel thought, if a man goes exploring, he cannot expect everything to work out according to plan. He told four men to stay with the boat.

'Bring the boat along the shore, as close to us as you can,' he said, 'only be careful that you do not get yourselves stranded.'

They waded ashore, keeping their shoes on, for at Tonga they had learnt of the poisonous stone-fish and the slow-healing cuts made by coral. The atmosphere was humid and the work was, therefore, doubly tiring.

Van der Lyn, the captain of marines, took charge of matters ashore. His men marched along the crest of a low dune and the seamen marched on the hard sand by the water's edge, with a small group of officers in between.

'This almost seems as if we are being too cautious,' said Isaac Gilsemans as he plodded through the sand beside

Francis Visscher. 'There's no evidence of anyone being about.'

'Only the evidence of the senses!' replied Francis. 'I can feel eyes at my back, peering out of every bush!'

'Just as you did in Van Diemen's Land, eh?' said Abel.

There was a clump of coconut palms to the north, and Abel made these their objective. As Isaac had said, there was no sign of people: no footprints in the sand or evidence of canoes having been hauled up. But he agreed with Francis, there was something in the air: a prickling sensation in the shoulder blades, which made every man turn round from time to time, just to see if something was there.

They reached the coconut palms and found clusters of ripening nuts among the leaves. Abel called one of the Javanese seamen to climb for them, and the man looped himself to the slender trunk with a loose girdle, then walked up it almost as fast as he could have walked along level ground. This feat never failed to fascinate the Dutchmen, and their attention was momentarily distracted as they watched the Javanese lean back against his girdle and slash the nuts with a parang.

Suddenly, as he looked down at the result of his work, he gave a cry of alarm: four long arrows quivered in the loam at the foot of the tree.

3

The Trepang Fishers

T H E marines turned in the direction from which the arrows had come. 'Rest your pieces!' called Captain van der Lyn, and the forked rests were planted firmly in the ground and the barrels levelled towards the scrub at the edge of the swamp. 'Present! Blow off your coals! Give fire!'

The glowing tips of the matches fell into the priming, and a volley crashed out. The buckshot crashed a swathe through the bush, and the marines went through the loading drill. Twenty seconds later a second volley crashed out, to be answered by yells of either pain or defiance.

'Back to the boats!' Abel ordered, sword in hand. 'Captain, can you cover a retreat?'

'Yes, commodore!' The marine told three men, 'You three, retire twenty paces and stand fast. Understand?' To the others he said, 'Right, men! A volley from you, then retire slowly twenty paces behind your mates. Ready? Give fire!'

As the attack began, the seamen rushed up the beach, gathered up the fallen nuts, then, cutlasses in hand, began moving to the water's edge under the command of Visscher. Abel stayed with the marines, whose volleys, four to the minute, covered the whole retreat. Howls from the bush answered each discharge, and the party were half-way to the water when the attackers burst over the crest of the dune. They were difficult to see, for their bodies were patterned with paint and ochre which blurred their outlines. They seemed to be thick-set and, between the Dutch and Javanese in size. Their hair was so decked and piled with feathers that they might have been wearing a wig.

Except at close range, buckshot does not kill, and the retreat continued as one group of marines leap-frogged past the other, turning to load and fire as their mates came back. Some of the yelling attackers fell or retreated; a marine was struck through the thigh with an arrow and a Javanese collapsed from the blow of a flung club. His ship-mates picked up the fallen man; van der Lyn attended to the marine. He snapped off the feathered end of the arrow and drew the stripped shaft through the wound almost before the man had noticed it. The man continued his firing, helping himself along with his musket-rest and, with a grin, refusing van der Lyn's proffered aid.

The boat was waiting a hundred paces from the shore, and Abel divided the party in two, in order to approach it from either end. Their attackers splashed into the water behind them and made for the smaller party. Abel had little doubt of their intentions. It was widely believed at that time that all the New Guinea people were cannibals, and that they were not only intent on killing the Dutch, but on carrying off the bodies to eat.

They drew closer to the boat, and the marines no longer had time to halt and load. The gunners' mate boarded and pressed the glowing end of a slow match against the priming of the swivel. The boat jerked back on the recoil as a kilo-gram of scrap-iron and gravel swept the ranks of the attackers. Without looking to see the effect of his shot, the cannoneer knocked out the wedges and reloaded. There was another howl as the second round was fired through the swirling smoke of the first.

Bodies lay awash in the shallows, and wounded warriors crawled or hobbled back to the shelter of the dune. The marines loaded with ball, and dropped long-shots among them to hurry them on their way. Some stopped and shouted defiance.

'Can you hear what they say?' Abel asked Jan Jorissen.

The interpreter shook his head. 'I can't recognize a word,' he confessed.

Abel smiled grimly. 'There must be more than one dialect in this land, then?'

'I think there are as many different ones as there are valleys, and I only learnt one.'

'It's lucky you are a good seaman. Why did you come as interpreter, if you realized you might be of no use? Oh, yes, there was trouble over a lady, wasn't there?'

'Two ladies, commodore. I was glad to get away.'

'Well, we need no interpreter to guess what they are saying on shore.' He looked round the boat, well afloat now in deeper water and pulling towards the *Bracq*. The marine who had been wounded was sitting up with a damp cloth round his head, and a smell of singed flesh told that the arrow wound had just been cauterized by burning a pinch of gunpowder on it.

'We have an artist on board. I'd like to take up one of those bodies so that he could make a drawing of it.'

'Not worth the risk,' said Francis, looking up from his rough surgery on the arrow wound. 'I, too, can draw, and you have a good memory. Between us we can give him all he needs to make a vivid picture.'

There was nothing to be gained by staying on a hostile shore, so they followed the coast to the east. The sea was very shallow, and a shadowy line on the larboard side was all that they could see of the land. A man was constantly in the chains taking soundings.

The lemons and onions they had brought were still sweet, and the water from Banda still good in the cask. There was enough rain, every day or so, for their needs, and Abel found it made better drinking water if one part in twenty of salt water was mixed with it. There was no sickness on board.

When it came to naming their landfall on the charts, Isaac said, 'Will you be calling this Murderers' Bay?'

'Why? No one was killed, and self-defence is no murder.'

'But we were attacked.'

'The attackers were only defending their land. We have met no murderers to compare with those of Staten Land. And I have my own idea as to why they were so hostile,' said Abel. 'It was quite possible they took us for Spaniards. All dark men look very much alike to us, and probably we all look the same to them. I've a mind to call this place Defiance Bay.' It was thus recorded on the charts, although later the name was changed.

On 21st March 1644 they found that the coast turned to the east. They were in the latitude where Torres had reported his strait, and Abel wondered if this could be its north shore. They decided to investigate. A good anchorage was discovered in the lee of a small island, and Abel and Francis transferred into the *Bracq*.

'There is plenty of timber over yonder,' Abel said to Dirk Haen, 'and you could set the hands to cutting wood and roasting charcoal while we are gone. We might set up a trade in turpentine, even if there are no spices.'

'And when shall I expect you back, commodore?'

'That depends on what we find. But we'll be away at least a week.'

Relieved of the duties of caring for a flotilla, Abel found the next few days a holiday. Jasper Koos was a good skipper, and the crew of the *Bracq* seemed to anticipate every order. Life in the galliot was pleasant, even if the quarters were cramped.

They had barely lost sight of their consorts when Abel began to doubt the existence of a strait. With leeboards down, the *Bracq* drew just over a fathom, and soon they were in a place where these ground and scraped constantly over coral, checking the little ship's way and jarring all on board. The weather was overcast and humid, so sights of sun or stars were impossible. Every afternoon rain squalls swept over the sea like dark cliffs. Breaks in rain or mist gave tantalizing sights of land, but they were never sure whether these were islands or coast.

Winds were very light and from the north-east. Often the sweeps were manned to clear the ship from the obtruding fangs of a reef. Francis knew that the running-chart he was making could only be approximately correct, yet he plotted his sightings as accurately as possible. One day he spoke with Abel about this chart. 'No one in the world could tell if there was a strait in this area. To be quite sure, a man would need wings to rise above the mists and eyes that could see through it!'

'I'm almost sure there's no practical strait, and Torres was wrong. We've touched the bottom with the *Bracq* a score of times, and if a galliot can touch the bottom, a ship would be stranded.'

Cautiously the *Bracq* withdrew from the labyrinth of coral, and after four days re-joined the other ships. In their absence, the anchorage had been surveyed and charted, ten quintals of charcoal roasted and a keg filled with sweet-smelling turpentine. Timber, unfamiliar to the carpenters, had been felled and was seasoning under damp sails in the 'tween-decks. They had seen no men, but the cooks had found several edible greens, as well as the ever present coconuts.

They sailed to the south-west, and on 27th March the lookouts sighted three sails. Suddenly they were in the middle of a great fleet of proas, ocean-going canoes used by the Malays.

'H'mmm! This could be the fishing fleet from a settled country,' said Francis.

'Yes, but they might have come a long way,' Abel reminded him, his eye to the telescope. One proa, larger than most, had flickered across the lens and something caught Abel's eye. Three buffalo tails fluttered from the peak of a sail, the sign of command used by some Malays. 'Close up on that proa, Francis, if you please. I think that is their admiral's ship. All precautions, of course, but I don't think they'll be needed.'

So the swivels were loaded and the boarding-netting rigged, with the gunners concealed under the high bulwarks. The two flotillas drew together, with the Dutch ships flying the States-General flag at the main. There were several men in the Dutch ships who understood the Malay language and they hailed the approaching proas. An elderly man, close-bearded and wearing the green-stranded turban of the Mecca pilgrim, balanced himself by the mast of the biggest proa and called back.

'I am Padukah of Johore, head of this fleet. Who are you, and why do you sail these waters?'

Johore! It was as Abel had thought, and these seamen were Malaysians who had sailed from a port even farther north than Batavia. He could forget about a wealthy city lying to the southward. But what were they doing here? Were they collecting pearls? It was possible, for the coral-strewn seas were said to be very like the Red Sea where the Arabian pearl fisheries were. It would please the merchants if they found a pearl fishery.

'I am Commodore Abel Tasman in the service of the Netherlands East India Company, of Batavia,' he replied through an interpreter. 'We seek a strait towards the east, reported by a Portuguese forty years ago.'

'You would believe a Portuguese, excellency? Sons of Shaitan that they are, they would tell lies in the face of Allah himself.'

'You know nothing of such a strait, tunku?'

'No man can, for such a strait does not exist.'

'Well! Is it permitted to ask why you come to these waters, tunku?'

'We have no secrets. We come to get trepang, the dried sea-cucumber, for which wealthy Chinese will pay a great price.'

'Good luck with the fishing! I am on a voyage of discovery, so I ask a question you may not care to answer.

What courses do you sail between Johore and this place?'

'We came through Malacca Strait into the Java Sea, then through Lombok Strait into the Timor Sea, and so to this place. We are two months out from Johore, and we make this voyage every year.'

Every year! If there was a strait to the east then a fleet such as this would have been almost bound to find it. Pure chance would have seen to that. But Abel's voice was calm as he asked, 'And how long have you and your people been making this voyage, tunku?'

There was no hesitation in the reply. 'Who can say? We come here each year, in my day and my father's day, and Allah alone knows how many years before that.'

They stayed two days with the trepang fishers, visiting the drying-racks where the ugly sea creature was prepared for the market. Abel wondered how a race as civilized as the Chinese could stomach such revolting-looking stuff.

'It takes all kinds to make a world,' he said to Isaac Gilsemans. 'If the Chinese will buy such food, you can't blame the Malays for supplying it.'

'It's a trade that's worth looking into,' replied Isaac, 'and there might be something in it for the company. Perhaps an all-year-round fishery on some island, manned by Javanese. I wonder how long the stuff keeps?'

'We'll make a note of it in the journal,' Abel said solemnly. 'As long as I'm not asked to carry it! Those proas smell worse than a Dutch crabber on a hot day!' He turned to Francis. 'Well, what do you think of Senhor de Torres and his strait?'

Francis shook his head. 'I don't know what to think, which doesn't mean that de Torres was lying. In shallow water among coral a lot of things can change in forty years, not to mention earthquakes and volcanoes.'

'Earthquakes? Volcanoes? What have they to do with it?'

'You must have heard a few years ago of the Smoking Island near Sumbawa?'

'I sailed by it once. It smelt worse than the trepang fleet, then—poof! It was gone.'*

'Well, Torres's account is clear enough, though I've only read it in translation. I believe he found a strait, but that since then it's become either choked with coral, or there's been an earthquake.'

'Then, Padukah may know something of it but is saying nothing for some purpose of his own.'

'That is hardly something you can enter in the journal. The fact is, if there is a strait, it lies to the east, the winds are dead foul, and the sea is choked with coral.'

'Head winds and coral reefs are sufficient reasons for not probing any farther,' said Abel. 'If there is a strait, it will be found from the eastward, and with favourable winds.'

* Such an island appeared in the Timor Sea about 1935, and was charted from the air and landed on by an aircraft. The following year it had vanished.

4
Limmen Bight

ANTHONY BLAUW set down the date and wrote in the journal as Abel dictated:

Having endured nothing but rain and head winds for the past fortnight we are satisfied that there is no practical strait to the east. We are off a coast in shallow water, with swampy shores and much coral. It is intended, if God wills, to follow this coast southward, to extend the discoveries made by Willem Jansz in the *Duyfken* forty years ago.

Abel looked round the council table. 'Are you all agreed on this? Has anyone anything to add?' He did not think he had a second Coomans with him, but he was taking no chances. 'Then we will all sign it, beginning with the most junior.'

Anthony Blauw signed first, Abel putting his own name at the end and adding a couple of fashionable flourishes. The visitors re-joined their ships, and the clink of capstan-pawls and the setting of headsails showed they were getting under way. Led by the *Bracq*, they headed south, heeling to the easterly breeze.

For a time, one day was almost exactly like another. The sun rose clear, but before it could dry out the dew-wet decks it was swallowed in cloud. Day after day the atmosphere was like that of a laundry where clothes are boiled, and many of the men itched and burnt in the torment of prickly heat. The wounded marine grew worse, his leg blackened and swelling in hideous ulcers, so that he eventually died of blood poisoning. His name was Carpentier—for he was of Huguenot stock—and they named a little river in his memory, not far from where he was buried at sea.

Francis made a running-chart as they went south, but the artist had an easy time; the coast was so barren there was nothing to draw. It rained often, but they did not drink the water. One thing the coast had was plenty of good water ashore.

'There must be a big country behind this coast,' Abel said one day, 'if we can judge by the size of its rivers.' A river showed its presence by a mud-stained sea, and sometimes the water was yellowed many miles out from the land. 'Somewhere there must be mountains where the sources of these rivers begin. But I've seen no sign of them yet.'

'Nor of villages or towns,' said Francis. 'And no sign of man, although the land looks arable enough. It's a big country, judging by the size of the rivers—maybe bigger than Van Diemen's Land. I cannot understand the absence of people.'

'Two Dutchmen have been here before: Jan Carstensz and Willem Jansz. Jansz saw no sign of man, but Carstensz did....'

Francis laughed. 'Carstensz was a bit of a blackbirder, I'm afraid. He tried to capture some people he found, to teach them Dutch and learn about their country. Only they did not like the plan—'

'And turned on him with spears! We shall have to see that this does not happen to us.'

They filled the water-casks three times on that coast, and each time the watering-party worked under guard, and the boats were armed with swivels. To some this seemed over-cautious, for on the first two occasions the white beaches were free of footprints, human or otherwise.

The third time they went ashore was different. It was not far from where Jan Carstensz had turned for the north, and on one beach there were footmarks, dead fires, empty shells and scattered fishbones. The footprints and fires did not look to be recently made, nor was there any sign of paths or a village. But signs of mankind were enough to make Abel take all precautions against attack. Marines stood guard with lighted matches while the seamen filled the casks in the river-bed. The guards and working party split in two halves, one filling casks in the river-bed and the other taking the filled casks down to the boats. They had then been working for about two hours and nothing had happened. Maybe they became a little complacent.

Suddenly a volley of flung spears and curved clubs hurtled from the scrub. The shower of missiles was accompanied by a dull roaring sound, but where it came from it was impossible to determine.

Abel and Francis had come ashore to stretch their legs, and Peter Paulsen, the artist, was with them. There was nothing for Paulsen to draw that would illuminate a chart, but he had conceived the idea of drawing some of the fantastic sea-creatures in the rock-pools along the shore, especially those that were edible.

At the sounds of combat the three turned to face the assault. Pistols in hand, they ran towards the noise. At first Peter ran too, but presently he sat on a driftwood log and began to draw on his sketching-pad. The water-carriers dropped their burdens and took up their flint-lock muske-toons, which were bell-mouthed for easy loading.

Five men fell at the first onslaught, but the bodies were recovered and their comrades surrounded them in a loose ring. Van der Lyn organized volley firing, and eight times a minute a thin volley of buckshot was discharged. The attackers kept their distance, and no one yet had used his cutlass.

The marines carried no cutlasses, but for a second weapon they had the bristle, the forked rest from which they fired their muskets. When a tall, black-bearded warrior, naked and patterned with daubed wood-ash and ochre, ran forward between two volleys, two marines dropped their firelocks, grabbed their rests from the ground and ran towards him.

The native poised a jointed spear, obviously with Captain van der Lyn in mind for a mark. One marine paused and flung his rest at the warrior, striking him under the breast-bone. The injured man, however, plucked out the rest and, shortening his grip on his stone-headed spear, ran at the second marine. Holding his rest quarterstaff fashion, the marine parried the spear thrusts, but the result would have been disastrous if his comrade had not regained his own rest and come to his assistance. Under their combined attack the black man turned and ran with a hand on the wound which was now streaming blood.

There was no further combat, and the attackers slowly withdrew under the steady volleys, into the scrub. The Dutch were able to breathe again, and take stock of the damage.

'Well, what's the extent of the injuries?' Abel asked his surgeon's mate an hour later.

'Two killed and seven wounded, commodore. On the other side, three killed and several wounded, some badly judging by the trail of blood they left. And some of our wounded will probably die in the night.'

'Two dead and seven wounded! That's a high price for a few kegs of water.'

Abel buried five men next day—three had died during the night—and was feeling depressed as he sat in the cabin after dinner.

'I suppose we have Carstensz and Jansz to thank for this,' he said. 'Curse them and their blackbirding tricks!'

'Carstensz maybe,' said Francis, 'but not Jansz. His *Duyfken* was a galliot like the *Bracq*, and a man can scarcely be warlike with no cannon and only a crew of fourteen.'

'Carstensz, then. He did try to take slaves, and the people he tried to rob haven't forgotten. Brave men, too; it's a pity they tried to kill us, because I'd have liked to see if Jan Jorissen could talk to them.'

Someone knocked on the door of the cabin.

'Come in!' Abel called, and in walked Peter Paulsen. 'I thought you might like to see the sketches I made of the fight yesterday, commodore.'

'Ah! You took some notes and worked them up later?'

'No, commodore. A number of these I drew on the spot. Some have been worked on later, of course.'

'You sat there *drawing* with all the fighting going on?'

'There wasn't much else I could do, commodore. I ... I had no weapon.'

Abel looked at him for a while, then laughed. 'No weapon!' he exclaimed. 'Well, at least being unarmed gave you time to draw.'

He untied the tapes of the portfolio and, with Francis by his side, leafed through the drawings. Peter had not seen the beginning of the attack, but his impression of what followed was vivid. The Dutch were in a circle round the bodies of their shipmates. Two seamen ignored a spilled cask, setting off weapons to aid the others. A marine stood, musket-rest poised to throw, facing an ochre-patterned enemy holding a raised spear. Two gentlemen, wheel-locks in hand, were depicted running towards the fight, and it was some time before Abel recognized himself and Francis. Had he really looked like that? He passed quickly, however, over the drawings of his shipmates to those of the natives, thin-shanked and heavily bearded, with their primitive arms. At last he turned to the artist.

'You have quick eyes, mynheer, and a rare talent for setting down what they perceive. See, Francis! These people are different from those who attacked us a month ago.'

'And why shouldn't they be, commodore? We have come as far from them as Norway is from Spain. It would be stranger if they were alike.'

'True enough, but where else in the world would you

find men so thin, so black, yet having such great beards? The merchants may think we have wasted time on this voyage, but the philosophers may be glad. Don't you see? We may have found a new race of men.'

'H'mmm! And had good Dutchmen killed to find them.'

'The price of discovery, Francis.' He turned to Peter Paulsen. 'Thank you for these drawings. I'll put them with the journal.'

'To place before the council? Let me touch them up first.'

'No!' Abel was firm. 'Not these! They are fine as they are, and one more scribe of the pencil might ruin them. Do another set—copy these if you wish—but these go to the council just as they are.'

Two days later they passed beyond the most southerly point marked by Jan Carstensz, and were again sailing in unknown seas. The coast turned almost due west; which made them sure they had sailed off the charts, for nowhere in his journal did Carstensz mention such a thing. This satisfied Abel, and all were pleased that the constant easterlies were now a soldier's wind, blowing from dead astern.

For eleven days they maintained a westward course, without incident, anchoring during the silent hours. These rests at night were welcome, for many of the men were sickly. Water was plentiful, but there was no fresh food, nothing but the store of pickled herring and pease-meal. Night lines were set for fish, but the small fish that took the bait became themselves bait for the bigger fish which broke the lines and made off. Stronger lines and traces were set, and these held sharks of such a size that they had to be shot before being hauled in. The carpenters flayed these and cured the hides, for shark leather is better than sandpaper for dressing wood. But no one could bring himself to eat the flesh of these maneaters.

On 6th May they upanchored after prayers. The weather had changed, and the long succession of grey days and lowering skies was almost forgotten. *Bracq* took the lead that morning, with the other ships following in line. Leadsmen were taking continuous soundings at ten-minute intervals, but the work was so exhausting that the man in the chains was relieved every hour. Isaac Gilsemans was concerned about this, for on the rocky bottom they had lost many leads and a good deal of line.

The day advanced, and the sun on the water became blinding. Not even the lookout saw the coral that ravaged *Limmen*'s bilge, though all felt it. The ship heaved as if in pain, her passage was checked, then she shuddered and resumed her course. Francis was on deck, and for a few moments thought that no damage had been done. Then he saw a length of teakwood sheathing heave out of the sea, astern, thrust an end into the air and slowly sink. Abel joined him as the last few spans disappeared.

'Don't tell me we've scraped the putty, because I felt that,' he said. 'What was that I saw sinking just now?'

'I hope it was a strip of the sheathing,' said Francis. 'I don't think it was planking, or we'd hear the water coming in.' He summoned the carpenter, and Peter Jacobs came to the poop. This was the same man who had swum ashore to set up the flag in Van Diemen's Land.

'You keep the deck, Francis, and I'll go below with Jacobs. If it's only cladding we've lost, we may be all right. Otherwise ...'

'I'll have a sail made ready to fother under the bottom,' Francis called after the commodore.

It was dark and humid in the orlop, but the air was fresh from the draught swept by the windsails down through the hatches. There was an ominous gurgle of water flowing, and from above came the squeal of the bos'n's call and the slap of bare feet on deck, as the watch mustered at the pumps. Loud splashing sounds came to their ears as a pail of sea water was tipped down the casing to prime them. It was difficult to see in the gloom, but they reached the source of the leak and Peter knelt down, exploring the damage with skilful fingers.

'How bad is it?' Abel asked, raising his voice over the racket of the pumps.

'Bad enough, commodore. The sheathing's gone, right enough, and the planking under it is shaved wafer-thin. You can see daylight at the seam.'

This was true, for in a space three spans long by half that width water was bubbling and a greenish glow of daylight showed on the upward roll. Abel inspected the damage to his ship and managed to conceal his anxiety.

'Maybe a sail fothered over it and plaster on the inside would fix it? We can shift the sail when the plaster sets.'

'A fothered sail, yes. But this gash is too big for a plaster plug.'

'Then we must careen her for repairs.'

Peter nodded. 'It's the only way. We're a long way from home.'

Abel rose and wiped his hands. 'We'll fother, and find a beach for careening. You'd better go and get the things you will need for the repairs.'

Francis was on the poop watching the mates as they supervised keel-hauling a spritsail over the bottom, to check the flow of water through the damaged strake.

'How bad is it?' he asked.

'She'll be all right for a day or two in this weather, but we're going to have to put her on the beach.'

'No chance of making Timor?'

Abel shook his head. The Portuguese had been on Timor for a century, but the Dutch were strangling their trade. It would be bad tactics to ask a favour of the Portuguese. 'It's five hundred and fifty leagues to Timor, and I don't want to be in debt to a Portuguese governor. We'll look for a clear stretch of beach, and heave her down.'

They were settling the sail over the damage now, and both men sighed with relief. 'It might have been worse,' said Francis. 'At least I'll be able to get the longitude and fix a new point of departure.'

There was no immediate danger, so long as they proceeded under easy sail and struck no more coral. Abel transferred to the *Bracq* and scouted ahead to find a beach, relying on the leeboards to give warning of reefs. He found what he was looking for on 8th May and went ashore in the *praam* to inspect it.

It was a not-too-gently shelving beach, with a sixteen-foot tide. There was a creek of fresh water, no sign of man, and apart from the insects it seemed ideal.

'What do you think, Mynheer Jacobs?' Abel asked the carpenter.

'We could go farther and fare worse, commodore.' Like many of his trade, Peter was inclined to pessimism.

'And that's God's truth,' said Abel, looking round the lonely shore. 'Nor do we have to seek far for a name. Limmen Bight will do very well.'

5

Birds, Swamp and Desert

WITH her topmasts down, and lightened of her load of stores, *Limmen* was floated up the beach at high tide until she rested over a clean stretch of sand. At the ebb she settled on the bottom, and was hove down on her side by means of tackles from the mastheads. Four hours after high water the carpenters had begun their repairs.

The cannon had been ferried ashore with the stores, and a stockade built with tents inside the ramparts, to shelter the crew. This took until the second day, and the carpenters said their work could not be completed in less than a week.

'All carpenters look on the black side,' said Abel. 'A week, and we've been here two days already.'

'Abel, you're compelled to idleness, and you don't like it,' said Francis, 'while I have the charts and the longitude to work on. If I may suggest it, why don't you make an excursion inland.'

'Now that's a good plan,' said Abel, who had not wanted to suggest it himself. He sought out the captain of marines, and found him with the master-gunner, drilling two teams on the four-pounders.

Abel came straight to the point. 'I have it in mind to make an excursion inland, mynheer,' he said, 'and I would like you to come with me.'

'Why certainly, commodore!' Van der Lyn had been hoping for this. 'How many marines?'

'Pick out your six fittest men. There'll be twice as many

seamen and five or six officers, with stores for four days. We'll set out tomorrow forenoon.'

'We're taking victuals for a four-day trek,' Abel said to Dirk Haen, 'but if we find anything edible we might be away longer. There seem to be plenty of birds, anyway.'

'I've never known of a bird you couldn't eat if you were hungry enough,' said the second in command. 'What are your instructions about a search party if you are not back in, say, a week?'

'There will be no search party: to search in this country would be to look for a needle in a haystack. If we do not return in seven days, you will wait one more week. I've set that down in writing, and it's countersigned by Mynheer Gilsemans, the chief merchant.' He handed over a sealed paper to Captain Haen. On it was marked *Not to be opened until 20th May 1644.*

'What is written here?'

Abel laughed. 'Something I hope you will never have to read, captain. They are your orders to return to Batavia, leaving a longboat and stores on the beach, well above the tidemark.'

'God forbid, commodore!' Dirk Haen did not think he could sail away leaving shipmates to an unknown fate in an unknown country.

'Don't worry, captain! *I* have no intention of sailing a longboat to Batavia.'

And I, thought Captain Haen, have no intention of leaving the coast without you. 'There's nothing more to say then, except to wish you all the best of luck.'

So Abel set out on his first expedition by land, unless his tramp on the hills of Fife so many years before in Scotland could be called an expedition. With him was Peter Paulsen the painter, Isaac Gilsemans the merchant, and Jan Jorissen the interpreter. There was van der Lyn and six marines, six Dutch and five Javanese seamen. The marines were armed with musketoons, for the eighteen-pound musket and its rest would be a heavy burden in tropical bush. The officers had sword and pistols and the others had kris or cutlass, according to inclination. And two of the Dutch seamen carried crossbows and quarrels, weapons they had made on board as a pastime during the dog-watches.

They floundered through the dunes, to find firmer footing in the thin scrub that lay beyond. This scrub was so thin that it was shadeless, yet without a compass it would have been impossible to keep direction. Progress was slow since it was easy for stragglers to lose the main party. It was far hotter than at sea, and the air was thick with insects. Shirts darkened with sweat, and the officers had difficulty in restraining the men from drinking the water in their canteens before they had been on their way for an hour.

It was not pleasant marching. As they continued, the ground became softer underfoot, and there was a new smell in the air: a stench that suggested a mixture of marigolds and sour bilges. They came upon a mangrove swamp, and the soft ground gave way to stinking slime, full of twisted roots. Only a hundred paces away they could see a pool of clean water, but whether this was lake or stream was difficult to tell. The surface of the water was thronged with thousands of birds of all sizes. There were slender-legged ones near the edge, which seemed to be able to run on the surface like waterbeetles, solemn waders going wisely about their business, pelicans with huge bills, ducks of many varieties, pied geese, while, overhead, hawks and eagles ranged; these must also have been preying on the fish, since none of the other birds seemed to heed their presence.

'So much for travelling by foot,' said Abel to Isaac Gilsemans. 'Now we must either hop through the mud like frogs, or swim like fish through the water!'

But between swamp and firm ground were clumps of bamboo, and given a cutlass and a bamboo grove a Javanese seaman can make anything from a hat to a house. Now they built rafts, and before sunset three of these lay in the water, moored to the mangroves. It had been a difficult task getting them there, and all involved had been in clinging mud up to the waist. They had seen centipedes as long as a man's forearm, and when the mud was washed off they found themselves covered with leeches. These looped along like caterpillars at first, then swelled to the size of a finger as they gorged on the blood. Abel felt a wave of horror when he found his body infested with these vile creatures, but the Javanese showed him how to get rid of them with either a twist of salt in a cotton rag, or a pad of wet tobacco. These caused the pests to drop away, but for a long time afterwards their victims bled from the tiny wounds. From that night on, they slept on the rafts, keeping insects at bay by burning smudge-fires in the cooking-pots.

For two days they explored this world of reeds and water, birds and insects. They poled and paddled from one lagoon to another, making portages over islets of firm ground, and the men became anxious that they might not be able to find a way back. But every change of direction was marked with a rag tied to a branch, or an axe-cut blazing the trunk of a tree. It was navigation by dead reckoning in a trackless swamp. There was no current or breeze, and Abel kept a tally by counting the steady paddle strokes. Peter Paulsen was a great help, for he sat facing astern, noting with a few quick pencil strokes the appearance of the bearing-marks as they would see them on their return. He also kept a record of the distance covered by the paddlers.

It was dull travelling, but there were consolations. The pied geese made good food, and the crossbowmen would knock these down with quarrels and only alarm a few at a time. There were eggs, and Abel learnt from the Javanese how to tell an addled one from a fresh one.

'Put them in a pot of water, tuan: if they sink they can be eaten. If they float...' The man held his nose in an unmistakable gesture.

'I'm not sure that a few rotten eggs wouldn't sweeten the air in these swamps,' said Jan Jorissen.

Apart from birds and insects, the only other living creatures they saw were crocodiles, but these seemed timid and afraid of man. But they were a nuisance, since they took many of the geese shot by the crossbowmen. Then the men thought of bringing down two at a time, paddling to the nearer one, with much commotion, and leaving the other to the swamp-dwellers.

After two days Abel decided to turn back, not daring to look for another way back to the coast in case they could not find a way out at all. The land seemed to consist of an endless chain of swamps and lagoons, with few dry places where a man could step ashore.

After more than one wrong attempt, they found their starting-point again, stripping the rafts to make footways through the mangrove swamp. Laden with pied geese and plastered with mud and leeches, they reached Limmen Bight in the late afternoon of 12th May.

Abel sat naked in the sea, rubbing the mud from his legs and watching the leeches shrivel and fall away. The tiny wounds bled, but the clean sting of salt water soon closed them. He then lay back for a long time, soaking the grime and fatigue of the past few days from his body.

Later, as he sat at a meeting in the stockade, with a smudge-fire burning and candles in sconces, he felt that the surroundings were almost civilized. 'I'm pleased to see the *Limmen* afloat again,' he said. 'The carpenters said it would be at least a week.'

'There's a carpenter for you!' said Dirk Haen. 'They always say double the time they think it will take, so that when they finish earlier we will think them supermen.' He flourished the drumstick he was eating. 'This is mighty fine goose. I've not tasted better anywhere.'

'Geese were the only good thing to eat we found,' replied Abel. 'We didn't try crocodiles, but we sampled most of the birds. Except for the ducks and geese, they all tasted of train-oil.'

'What was the land like, commodore?' asked Anthony Blauw. 'Were there any chances of trade?'

'We never reached land, unless you can call a mangrove swamp by that name. I could see no chance of trade at all.'

Francis spoke up. 'I've heard of places on the Slave Coast of Africa rather like this, with dunes and mangrove swamps fringing the shore. But rivers flow into the mangroves, and a few days' sail upriver will bring you to the towns.'

'So, what we must find is some great river leading into the interior,' said Abel.

'That's a good thought,' said Isaac Gilsemans. 'Come to think of it, Egypt is like that. A cousin of mine in the Levant trade told me of it. Seaward, he says, is a desolate shore, fringed with the ruins of cities like Alexandria and a few fishing villages. But a few days' sail upstream—if you can find the stream!—and you come to Cairo and all the wealth of the East. Slaves, gold-dust, gums, ivory, ebony, ostrich plumes—you name it! A good trader can make his fortune there in two years.'

'Or be as dead as a doornail in one!' said Abel. 'As I've heard, Egypt has more plagues and poxes than three Javas put together. But as soon as we get *Limmen* re-rigged and stored again, we'll go looking for this river to lead us to Tom Tiddler's ground.'

In after years Abel often thought of the dreamlike quality of this present voyage, since there were not the contrasts in weather or events, as there had been in the previous voyage, to divide the trip into periods. For after the second encounter with natives everything seemed to merge into a long dream. They sailed and sailed, charting island and mainland, bay, sound and gulf; all of them vague and featureless. Sometimes there were beaches, and sometimes the mangroves stood rooted in the sea with oysters growing on them. Once they had penetrated a deep gulf, named on the charts for Anthony van Diemen, and they hoped that it would lead into the great river they were seeking. It was now the middle of June.

'That inlet to the south,' said Abel, in the evening when they had anchored for the night, 'could well be the mouth of a river.' It was the most promising landfall they had made for weeks, with a wide inlet and a hint of hills in the country to the south. 'I'd like you to take a party ashore this time,' he went on, speaking to Francis Visscher. 'You and Isaac Gilsemans. Maybe a change of leader will change the luck.'

'But my charts! The determination of longitude?'

'The charts can wait a while, and Haen and I will compute the longitude. You can arm the longboat and be off in the morning to find Isaac another grand Cairo.'

So the longboat made for the inlet, with a swivel mounted at the bow and four marines as an armed escort. Astern of it bobbed a string of empty water-casks, for there had been no rain for some weeks and there would certainly be fresh water if they could pull the boat beyond the tide limit.

The ships took advantage of the pause by running the guns across from side to side, so that when they heeled the bilges were exposed and could be cleaned of barnacles and weed. For this work the men used long-handled scrubbers and scrapers. Even though *Limmen* and *Bracq* had been beached and breamed at Limmen Bight, the seagrass had grown as long as the grass in a summer meadow. All the rigging was made good, while the boys were sent with the *praam* to gather oysters from the mangrove roots. These made a tasty chowder with biscuits and salt pork.

The shore party returned after three days, towing the filled water-casks. The wide inlet had dwindled after some distance to a creek, and while the casks were being filled, Francis and Isaac, accompanied by two marines, had made a three-hour march to the south.

'And saw no sign of grand Cairo?'

'We saw no sign of anything,' replied Isaac. 'Once we had hopes, when we found the ashes of a fire. But it was a whole tree burnt down, so we think it might have been struck by lightning.'

'And we saw a pack of dogs running in the distance.'

'No, Francis! You know we did not agree on that. I thought the creatures were more like large birds.'

Abel laughed. 'Come, shipmates! Fur and feather cannot be so alike!'

'Truly, I thought they were dogs from their size.'

'And I thought them more like large fowls, running with outstretched heads,' said Isaac.

'Couldn't you tell by the legs?'

'That's just what we couldn't do. As they ran, they raised so much dust that we couldn't see their legs at all.'

The days went by, and they traced a coast that trended south, west, then south-west. After that they traced two hundred leagues of barren and waterless desert shore. There were gulfs and islands they could not sail close to, for there were shoals and coral reefs.* At 18° south a landing was made near an inlet, but it only led to a dry creek-bed, while the hinterland was stony wilderness as far as the eye could see. On 1st July 1644 Abel summoned his council.

'We have a decision to make,' he said. 'Water is beginning to run short, and we must decide whether to push on, hoping to find some, or turn back before we die of thirst. The pilot-major will tell us what is known of this coast to the south, to help us make up our minds.'

Francis Visscher had drawn a rough chart in charcoal, and this was pinned to the bulkhead. He was not the only one to see a resemblance between the coast he had drawn and that of a rough-haired hound. 'We all know of our own discoveries,' he said, 'and, as far as I know, we are the first to report them, ever since before we came to Limmen Bight. But others have found what I believe to be the south-

---

* Parts of the north-west Australian coast are shown in dotted lines on largescale charts to this day.

ward part of this coast, and I will recall them in order. The first was Dirk Hartog, in the *Eendracht*, thirty years ago. He was bound from the Cape of Good Hope for Batavia, when he was driven off-course by a gale. He sighted land in 26° south, and was lucky not to be driven ashore by the storm. He held north, making what easting he could, until he reached the Tropic of Capricorn. Then the wind shifted, and he bore away for Java.'

'Very sound of him to do so,' said Isaac Gilsemans. 'Honest trade must always come first.'

There was a rumble of laughter, and Francis continued. 'Two years later Pieter Dirkszoon of the *Zeewolf*, and Willem Jansz of the *Mauritius*, sighted a cape in 22° south within two months of one another. Jansz sent a boat ashore to look for water, but he had the same kind of luck as we are having: he didn't find any.'

'Frederick de Houtman sighted land in 28° south, and that was a desert coast, too—'

'In fact,' interrupted Jasper Koos, 'what you are telling us is that there are hundreds of miles of desert coast. Is that right?'

'Near enough. We've found mangrove swamp as far as 14° south, and a desert coast from there to 30° south. Every captain, but one, says the same. I am sorry I am unable to tell you that captain's name—I cannot find it mentioned anywhere.'

'Tell us what you do know, Francis,' said Abel.

'Well, the ship was the *Leeuwin*, and she reported the most southerly sighting of all in 1622. They saw a high cape in 35° south, with land trending away to the east.'

'Well, a cape makes a good change after all this flatness,' said Jasper Koos.

'It did them little good, because they could no more find a landing than we could at the Three Kings Islands. There were high seas and a surf breaking against the foot of the cliffs. But it was not a desert coast, for they saw trees growing on the cliff-tops, and there were flowers in the clefts of the rocks.'

'And that's all?' asked Captain Haen.

'That's all. This coast has been sighted at intervals from 22° to 35° south by others, and we've traced it from the north to where we are now, between 20° and 21° south. And the question is: do we go south, knowing almost certainly what we will find, or do we bear away for Sunda Strait and Batavia?'

There was not much discussion before the votes were cast. No one was for going on, and the decision was recorded in the journal and signed by everyone.

On 5th August 1644 three salt-caked ships, riding high out of the water, passed Sunda Strait and finally came to anchor in Batavia Roads. Abel Tasman had come home again.

6

Back to Honest Trade

'TYPICAL Batavia weather!' growled Abel, stripping off his oil-silk cape and hat, and handing them to the Javanese steward. 'The governor wished to see me, Adam. Is he free?'

'He is waiting for you in his workroom, tuan.'

Abel was shocked when he saw van Diemen. Like many of the company's servants, the governor suffered from occasional bouts of fever, and he had not been a well man when Abel had sailed eight months before. Now, his yellowed skin was stretched tight over sharp cheekbones, and he greeted his caller with a ghostly smile.

'Thank you for coming so promptly, Abel. I thought it would be as well to have a talk before the council met.'

'I brought a copy of my journal, mynheer. It is the same as that which will be tabled at the council meeting, except—'

'Except that it will have one or two private notes in the margin, eh?' There was that deathly smile again, as the yellowed fingers riffled through the pages. 'I'll read this before council meets, of course, but there are a few things I'd like to know from you personally. What about Torres's strait, for instance?'

Abel hesitated. 'We—the pilot-major and I—doubt if the strait exists.' The governor looked up sharply, and Abel said, 'A practical strait, that is.'

'What do you mean, commodore?'

'I mean a strait that could be negotiated by a ship of size, not a channel that could only be used by canoes or boats.'

'So there may still be a strait.'

'I cannot say there is not. And if there is, it will not be found from the west.'

'Ah, yes! The prevailing wind is from the east, of course. Tell me more.'

Abel tried, but he knew he could not do this sort of thing well. He was not an orator who could sway a hostile council. He spoke of grey days during the monsoon, with sea and sky merging into a leaden blur; of grey-green seas creaming into surf over hidden reefs, or bursting upwards like cannon-shot against exposed rock; of the shuddering rumble as *Bracq*'s leeboards scraped the coral, and of the steady easterlies that kept blowing them off-course.

'I see your difficulty. Yet you still think there might be a strait?'

'It's possible, but it would have to be sought from the east. I think Torres told the truth. He was sailing from the east, after all.'

'If—and I say if—you had to sail again to look for this strait, how would you set about it?'

'I've thought a lot about that, mynheer, and there's only one way and it could take two years. Perhaps more.'

'Go on.'

'The east coast of New Holland must be found first.'

'That is what I hoped you might do in your first voyage.'

'Maybe you did. But my hands were tied with instructions either to find a route to Chile, or search for a coast westward from the Solomons or Tonga.'

'That was the council's doing, not mine.'

'They were still orders I had to carry out.'

'And if you had been a free agent, what then?'

'I'd have continued north along the coast of Van Diemen's Land, and seen what it had to offer. From what I know now—it's in the journal there—there must be a great land to the north, with New Guinea at the head of it.'

The governor rose painfully and looked at a chart on the wall. 'I've had this drawn since you left,' he said. 'You'll note that it has *my* land and Staten Land shown. Now let me see. Why, from Van Diemen's Land to New Guinea is at least a thousand leagues!'

'That's why I say it will take two years or more. We simply don't know what we will find, and it could take six months to get to Van Diemen's Land just to make a start. I've followed twelve hundred leagues of new coast in the last seven months, I know, but I did have favourable winds for much of the way. On the east coast I don't know what I might find.'

'And you think that's the only way to find this strait? For, if it exists, it will be of great value when we open up trade with the isles of the Pacific Ocean.'

'If Torres found a strait, he found it from the east. I'm convinced about that. And that's the only way from which it can be proved, until someone invents a ship that can sail dead into the wind!'

Both men laughed heartily at the absurd notion. The governor said, 'Would you sail on another voyage to find this strait, on the route you've suggested?'

'To have those armchair seamen on the council cry down my findings as they did before? What do you think, mynheer?'

'I don't recall they cried down your findings, so much as the fact that no new openings for trade were disclosed.'

'I was not to blame for that. I cannot create cities on a barren coast, or discover men where there are none.' He took the cup of punch the governor offered and drank from it. 'I think I am done with exploring, mynheer. If you want a new expedition, let Jasper Koos or Dirk Haen lead it. Both are good men and deserve a chance to make a name for themselves.'

'They might make a great name for themselves if New Holland is at all like Africa. Look at the wealth the Portuguese found on that east coast.'

'I'm not sure we should press the resemblance of New Holland to Africa too far, mynheer. There are rich cities on the north and west coasts of Africa—Tunis and Tangier—

as well as Mozambique and Mombasa on the east. We found *nothing* along twelve hundred leagues of coast. It could well be that New Holland is a desert continent, lacking both cities and men.'

There was a silence, except for the sighing of the punkah as it stirred the humid air. 'Abel,' said the governor, 'do you realize we had almost quarrelled? Fill that cup and light your pipe. Relax.'

'Gladly,' said Abel, leaning back in his chair. He had not yet recovered his land-legs, and the effort of walking on solid ground tired him. During the last weeks of the voyage there had been a shortage of water, and they had not eaten fresh food for two months, since June, when they had taken the oysters from the trees. His joints ached as a result, and his teeth loosened. He was thirsty for the punch, more for the acid lime juice than the good Dutch gin it was made with. Since coming ashore he had been almost greedy for fruit and meat.

'I'll accept the fact that you do not want to go on another voyage of exploration, Abel. Not even to set up a trading-post on a share basis with the company if you found the right place.'

'The right place!'

'Well, you might become very rich that way, very rich indeed, and it would prove to those who say—'

'Those who say what, mynheer?'

'Those are not my words, nor my thoughts. But it has been said that you do not press on as far as you might, that you could be more persistent—'

'In fact, that I lack courage?'

'Not exactly that, either. Let us say they think you are overcautious.'

Abel laughed bitterly. 'That's a fine way of calling a man a coward! Tell me, what are the reasons for the voyages I have made?'

'To find out new things and to make them known to other men.'

'Agreed! And how are these new things made known?'

The governor nudged the canvas-bound journal on his table. 'By journals such as this, and the charts made from your observations.'

'And if the ship and crew are lost, what then?'

'If the ship and crew are lost? Yes, I get your point. In other words, it is important that the explorer returns.'

'Especially from an otherwise unknown coast. In all later voyages the explorer has a starting-point at least. The first discoverer must be bold enough to make his find, then prudent enough to take no unnecessary risks to get back and tell about it.'

The governor was impressed. 'Please go on, Abel. You have become quite a philosopher.'

Abel swallowed another half-cup of deliciously acid punch before he spoke again. 'Last voyage I charted twelve hundred leagues of new coast. From Cape Valsh in New Guinea to Cape Leeuwin in New Holland there are only forty leagues not set on the chart. I *could* have surveyed that last forty leagues—I know that—but to do so would have been to risk both ships and men.'

'So you turned back while you could, in order to bring back your report?'

'I did, and if any accuse me of overprudence after that—'

'No one will say that in my presence, Abel.'

'I have risked much to find out what I have, mynheer. Others at least know where to begin looking.'

'I assure you that your courage is not in question, commodore.'

'Not by you, mynheer, I am certain of that. But there will be plenty to whisper it behind our backs. Three times I've sailed into unknown seas, the first voyage being with Commodore Quast. I've taken a lot of chances, and I've been lucky. Only a fool pushes his luck too far.'

'You intend swallowing the anchor?'

'I didn't say I would not sail again, only that I'd not explore again. I've been at sea too long to want to live ashore, but when I sail next time, it will be in the way of honest trade, to try and make a little gold for myself.'

He rose and prepared to leave. 'There's the journal, your excellency. Twelve hundred leagues of new coast. I wear a sword, and I'd be glad to hear of any who dub me over-cautious—'

The governor interrupted sharply. 'I'll not have the *duello* in Batavia, commodore. Sword-fighting can be left to the Spaniards who invented it!'

'I'm no dueller, governor. But I consider I've the right to use the flat of my blade across a slanderer's backside?'

The governor laughed, his ravaged face a pitiful sight. 'I plan to visit the Netherlands next year, and goodness knows what trouble you will get yourself into while I'm away. See that you don't get involved in any lawsuits— lawyers are worse to deal with than duellers.'

Abel made a formal bow. 'I'll bear that in mind, mynheer. And I am truly sorry that you plan to leave us.' Privately he thought the governor had no chance of ever seeing the Netherlands again. 'May I say there is nothing whatever against yourself in my decision not to go exploring again.'

'Abel, I know that. Often I'd like to throw away my governorship and get back to honest trade myself.'

Afterwards

IN October 1644 Abel's pay was increased to one hundred guilders a month, backdated to August 1642.

Anthony van Diemen died in April 1645, and after his death no further expeditions were sent to explore New Holland for many years.

In 1645 and 1646 Abel made several voyages to Ceylon, publishing, in the latter year, a book of navigational aids for the passage from Batavia to Colombo. Later in 1646 he voyaged to Sumatra, forestalling a rival English company in buying up the whole of the pepper crop.

In 1647 he headed a trade mission to Thailand, signing a treaty with the king for a trade concession on tin and timber.

Now we come to the most controversial action in his career. In 1648 he was appointed admiral of a fleet of eight ships which sailed in April to attack Spanish posts in the Philippines. In August he successfully attacked the Babuyan Islands, north of Luzon. The islands were in a very unsettled state, and Abel ordered that there was to be no shore-leave from the fleet. He and his second in command were obliged to go ashore for a meeting with the Spanish governor, taking with them an armed guard. Returning to the ships, they disturbed two young Dutch sailors who had disobeyed the order and stolen ashore to collect loot.

Abel tried them on the spot and sentenced them to be hanged. However, he pardoned them after they had been hauled up with ropes round their necks, cutting one of them down with his own hand. He declared he only wanted to teach them a lesson, and that the next offenders would be left hanging. This seems a very severe punishment, but we must consider it against the background of circumstances. Even today 'To desert his post of duty in an active theatre of war' would be an offence leading to court martial and could result in a sentence of death.

On returning to Batavia, Abel faced a Court of Inquiry into this action. He was found guilty of exceeding his duty, suspended from office, and ordered to pay compensation to the sailors. He was reinstated in his command in September 1650.

About this time his daughter Claesgen married Philip Heylman, a surgeon. She had one son, who was named Abel. Dr Heylman died in 1655; Claesgen later married a man named Breemer.

Also in 1650 Abel Tasman sold the house he owned in Amsterdam, and a survey of Batavia the same year shows that he owned two hundred and eighty-eight acres of town land. He resigned from the Dutch East India Company in 1652, and bought a ship to go trading on his own account.

He made a will in 1657, but the exact date of his death is unknown. He was almost certainly still alive in 1659, but it is probable that he died before 1661. Jannetie Tasman later married a man named Bridger, and returned to the Netherlands. There is some evidence that the Bridgers re-emigrated from there to Bradford, in Yorkshire.

We do not know what Abel Tasman looked like. There is a picture of a man, woman and girl in the National Library of Australia which is said to be the Tasman Family, attributed to Jacob Gerritz Cuyp (1592-1651). Many experts doubt that Cuyp was the painter, or that the Tasmans were the subject.

We know that he must have been physically tough and disciplined, that he was a fine seaman and a good navigator. Had he not been, he would not have been sent on three voyages of discovery. He must have had a reputation for physical courage, or in those days of boarding-parties and hand-to-hand combat he would never have been given command of a fleet in war in 1648. Yet he had detractors who accused him of overprudence, in spite of the fact that he charted thousands of miles of hitherto unknown coast-line. Some of this has not been properly surveyed to this day, and other parts are avoided by ordinarily prudent seamen except when absolutely necessary.

It would almost seem as if his rivals in the company tried to suppress his work. Including his own journal, several copies of accounts of his first Australian voyage exist, but no accounts at all of his second. Only in the past century has his work come to be recognized, and his first discovery was renamed Tasmania in his honour in 1853. The third section of this book is a reconstruction of Tasman's second Australian voyage, derived from a study of the Batavian Council's orders for the journey, and a study of maps of the period. All the incidents are based on fact.

Some Historical Notes
The Revival of Learning and the Reformation took place in the late fifteenth and early sixteenth centuries, and one result of the first was a wave of geographical exploration. It began with Columbus (A.D. 1446-1506) and Vasco da Gama (1460-1524) and ended in 1911 when Amundsen and Scott reached the South Pole.

Between 1492 and 1750 almost all exploration was made for purposes of trade, although the earlier ones were some-times masked by a religious excuse. Actually the explorers sought gold or slaves, or new markets or better routes to existing ones.

The Reformation caused a century of religious wars, from A.D. 1550 to 1650. One of the longest of these was fought by the Spanish and the Dutch in the Netherlands between 1568 and 1648. During this period the Dutch people turned from a farming and fishing economy to the high seas, at first almost as pirates and later as traders. About 1600 the

Netherlands East Indies Company was formed, and quickly expanded into a great trading empire.

At the same time the English East India Company began, in opposition to the Spanish and Portuguese, who were already established in Asia. A series of trade wars began, quite unconnected with the religious wars in Europe. By 1640 Spanish power had waned except in the Philippines, and all that remained to Portugal was part of Timor, Macao in China and Indian Goa. The English were extending in India proper, while the Dutch held much of what is now Indonesia and had a toehold in South-east Asia, China and Japan.

What Anthony van Diemen sought when he sent Abel Tasman on his travels was not scientific fact or land suitable for settlement, but new markets to offset the possible loss of those in China and Japan. Compared with voyages from Europe of the sixteenth and seventeenth centuries, Tasman's voyages of ten and seven months seem short. But he started from Batavia, which was a passage of between six and eight months from the Netherlands, and which was itself on the fringe of an unknown world. To do what he did from Europe, Tasman would have had to make voyages of two and a half to three years.

Dutch shipbuilding of that time was the best in the world, but even so *Heemskerck* or *Limmen* were crude by modern standards. A sailing ship of today, especially a racing yacht, can perform feats of sailing into wind that would not have been believed by seamen of the seventeenth and eighteenth centuries. Gear was heavy, and there was no power available to handle it except human muscle, so large crews were essential. Ships were crowded, and food, except for the first few days at sea, was poor. Captains in tropical waters lived in constant dread of a mutinous crew taking the ship and marooning or murdering the after-guard. Many a pirate owed his start in the trade to a successful mutiny.

In 1642 there was still much to discover in the South Pacific, and Tasman has been criticized for finding so little.